James Gould Cozzens   Selected Notebooks: 1960-1967

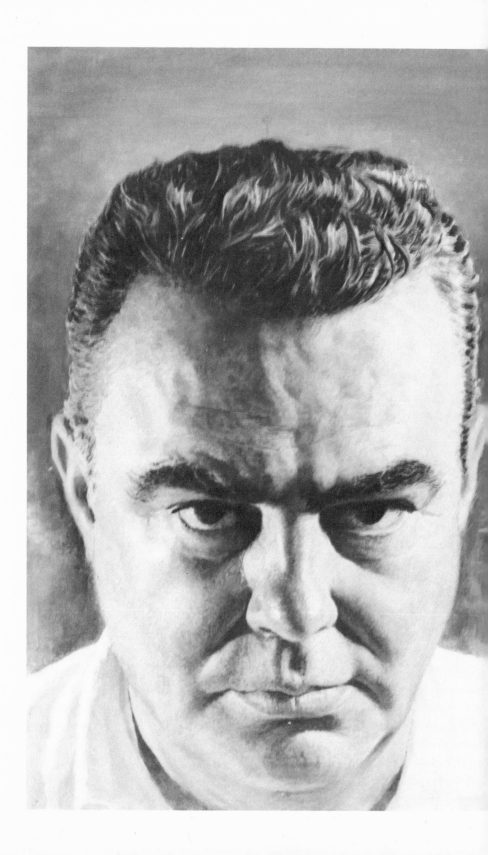

James Gould Cozzens

Selected Notebooks: 1960-1967

Edited by Matthew J. Bruccoli

 Bruccoli Clark Publishers
Columbia and Bloomfield Hills
1984

Acknowledgments   I am indebted to the excellent staff in the Princeton University Library Manuscripts Department: Richard Ludwig, Jean Preston, Mardel Pacheco, Charles Greene, Ann Van Arsdale, Barbara Taylor. Schuyler Hollingsworth, Recording Secretary of the President and Fellows of Harvard College, made it possible for this volume to be published. Catherine Coleman assisted me in the early stages of editing, and Judith Baughman worked with me on the preparation of setting copy.   M.J.B.

Contents Introduction ix

The publication of *By Love Possessed* in 1957 brought fifty-four-year-old James Gould Cozzens welcome money and unwelcome notoriety. He became briefly famous for his refusal to behave like a celebrity. Although his previous novels had attracted attention in the form of Book-of-the-Month Club selections and a Pulitzer Prize for *Guard of Honor*, he had been able to maintain his aloofness from the literary life and its controversies. But it was open season on the author of *By Love Possessed*. He was the subject of a *Time* cover story in which his self-directed irony irritated readers. The initial admiring reviews of the novel were followed by a counter-assessment, notably Dwight Macdonald's "By Cozzens Possessed" in *Commentary*.

Cozzens attempted to protect his reclusive writing life and get on with his work. After selling their Lambertville, New Jersey, farm in 1957, the Cozzenses moved to the eastern shore of Virginia and then in 1958 bought "Shadowbrook" outside Williamstown, Massachusetts. He began a novel to be called "A Skyborn Music" which was abandoned for *Morning Noon and Night*. The novel went slowly; it was not published until 1968. Driven by his habit of writing every day — which had become a need — Cozzens began keeping notebooks in 1960. At various stages of his life he had maintained detailed diaries, but the ten Williamstown notebooks for 1960-1967 are the only such documents that he preserved. They include observations on writing and the literary profession, notes on his reading, broodings on life and death, comments on current events, and autobiographical memoranda. He later explained to his publisher William Jovanovich:

Though dated items, in them's no kind of 'diary' or 'memoir' notion; only a collecting, hodge-podge and planless, of thoughts on stuff I read, or heard, or watched happen that I could see as coming in handy in some future fiction I might write — a few passages in Morning Noon & Night *did* come from one or another of these notes. As they get on, mixed in them at random though not at all by chance are some quite unpublishable carefully detailed settings-down of personal experience. The reason — I'm sure your discernment will have told you before I confess it — was dismay come suddenly in these years at realizing beyond question that my memory, the only part of me that was Achilles but unappreciated, taken for granted in its close to photographic capacity, was faltering, must soon, like any old man's, begin serious forgettings or worse misrememberings. Thus past episodes for some reason brought to mind, had best if I hoped to use them someway, be put in writing while I could be sure the fact remembered really was fact. I can tell you this was damn dismaying, ego wounding, I suppose.[1]

One subject that veins his notebooks is Cozzens's sense of being all out of fashion in contemporary letters; but he was certain that the prevailing fashions were cheap. Although he insisted that he was indifferent to criticism, he had been wounded by the attacks on *By Love Possessed*. His reaction was not so much anger that his work had been disparaged as a sense that he had been personally sullied by the animadversions of people he regarded as critical "nuts" and "queers." Cozzens frequently reminded himself that the wages of authorship include abuse; nonetheless, he regarded his work as his own, and he didn't want *them* fingering it or him.

In his seclusion Cozzens failed to perceive how much the world outside his study had changed. Remarks that seemed unobjectionable to him were outrageous to other people. Thus he commented to the *Time* interviewer about his thirty-year marriage: "I suppose sex entered into it. After all, what's a woman for? . . . Mother almost died when I married a Jew, but later on when she saw I was being decently cared for, she realized that it was the best thing that could have happened to me."[2] Born in 1903 and educated at a High-Church prep school, Cozzens retained the presuppositional biases of his caste that made him seem an anachronism. He regarded Catholics and Jews as foreign importations; Roman Catholic doctrine — as explicated in *By Love Possessed* — demeaned its practitioners; liberals were "boneheads" or "soreheads."

Since some of his prominent detractors were Jews and since the Macdonald attack had appeared in *Commentary* (which styled itself "a journal of significant thought and opinion in Jewish affairs and contemporary issues"), Cozzens came to classify all liberal intellectuals as Jews. Yet he insisted that he was not anti-semitic:

I know that any — well, pontificating, on the subject of yourself is always shaky. You don't see yourself. Yet, in a strange sense, you *feel*

1. 8 August 1976. Harcourt Brace Jovanovich.
2. "The Hermit of Lambertville," *Time*, CXX (2 September 1957), 72-74, 76, 78.

yourself, and I know I wouldn't be anti-anybody by category or class for the bad (not good) reason that this would involve by definition some subscribing to or standing on principles. I don't give a hoot in hell about the race, color, religion of individuals. All I go by is whether I find this one agreeable — or, in short: if he be not bad to me, what care I how bad he be? (28 November 1964).

In a 1970 letter to William Jovanovich, Cozzens commented on his notebooks: "I think I am not wrong in saying some of it is quite good. Under the title of, say, Intents and Purposes I can see the possibility of bunching the stuff in several categories: e.g. Doubts & Difficulties; What happened Then; Are we Crazy? This is not a proposal."[3] By 1975 Cozzens was at Rio, Florida, and had stopped writing. Jovanovich, concerned by Cozzens's deepening anhedonia, proposed that the Williamstown notebooks be published — partly to keep Cozzens's name before the public and partly as bibliotherapy. Cozzens reluctantly agreed to consider the plan and arranged for the holograph notebooks to be transcribed by a graduate student in the Princeton University Library, where they had been deposited. A Harcourt Brace Jovanovich contract was prepared and an editor was assigned to the volume; but Cozzens's wife, who was his agent, dissuaded him from continuing with the project because she felt that publication of the notebooks would expose him to renewed partisan abuse. A sampling from the notebooks was appended to the biography *James Gould Cozzens: A Life Apart* (1983), and the response prompted the present volume.

Cozzens wrote major novels in the Thirties, Forties, Fifties, and Sixties, leaving a body of fiction unsurpassed in its fidelity to experience:"To me, life is what life is."[4] A gauge of his achievement is provided by the frequency of *best* in descriptions of Cozzens's work: the best American novel about the law; the best American novel about World War II; the best American novel about the ministry. If the fatigued honorific *master* has any value as a critical term, it applies to James Gould Cozzens's lifetime of refining his techniques as a means for accurately representing experience to grown-up readers. His hard-learned lessons on the writing life merit the attention due a master.

3. Princeton University Library.
4. *Time*, 78.

James Gould Cozzens
Selected Notebooks: 1960-1967

Editorial Note   To select is to distort. The principle of selection for this volume was to retain most of the entries dealing with the practice of literature and to omit most of the entries in which Cozzens commented on the news or quarrelled with religious activities. Except where stipulated, the entries are complete. There are no silent emendations; Cozzens's spelling and punctuation have been transcribed as exactly as his difficult handwriting allowed. (His semi-colons and colons and his brackets and parentheses cannot always be differentiated.) The mentions of "S." refer to Sylvia Bernice Baumgarten Cozzens, his wife.

1   1 April 1960-23 December 1960

IV 60   Plotonius' 'flight of the alone to the alone' must have seemed to him, as well as a possible description of the mystical state an admission of its unmeaning from the standpoint of reason

"I wish I loved the Human Race
I wish I loved its silly face . . ." Anon

IV 3   the habit, common to most men, of compartmenting their lives. As in the history of Solomon Grundy, sufficient to a day are the doings of a day

IV 4   the obviousness of Hamlet's: 'What a piece of worke is a man . . . and yet — '

IV 10   that basic imperception which makes him able, half intellectually snobbish, yet half credulous and uncertain, to find 'literature' in the word games of James Joyce

that many men, if they have power, find they can easily do without most other gratifications

IV 12   The average fair-minded person is inclined to be 'liberal' for the chief reason that he can't but see that conservatism, however plausible its arguments, must boil down to a declaration by those who are top-dog that it's good and right for them to remain top-dog.

IV 13   Writers who ask a good deal of the reader. I don't mean in the factitious guessing games about symbolism or levels of meaning of the little magazines but in point of adult experience and a grown-up mind. If, for reasons of partisan anger, or arbitrary doctrinaire critical concepts, he doesn't feel like giving a good deal; or if, in fact, he doesn't happen to have much to give, he will naturally find the too-demanding work a bad one
— those who were put off it for various partisan reasons and so didn't feel like giving a good deal

IV 17   Dispassionately viewed, the charges were neither fair not presented in a fair way so they would carry weight only with people whose partisan feelings, pitched close to hate or fury, resolved them to find both him and his work bad.

IV 20   those overwhelming emotional discoveries: half eternal truth, half nonsense (Je suis ton maître et ta proie)

IV 29   apathies of inexpectation, no play ahead, no fun looked forward to, nothing wished for

IV 30   In the days of the silent movies they used to have a device to indicate passing time. The leaves of a daily calendar rippled quickly by and in half a minute weeks had passed. Getting older, every man must come to realize that this quick ripple of sheets is the actual fact, that just so his time, his life, *does* pass

V 9   there is an unlovely part of our human nature that makes a man find the success of his friends nearly as insupportable as the success of his enemies

V 14   the fact remains that James Joyce is pretty hard going unless you're supported by the satisfaction of being able to think: here I am, reading like anything and highly appreciative, what hardly one reader in ten thousand can manage to read. Would a cult of — say — the Congressional Record; or of grammar school 'themes' be ruled out?

V 16   the moments of ordinary ambivalence; odi et amo: the mixed feelings of anxiety in joy and, more mysteriously, joy in anxiety

V 24   It asks a good deal of the reader. He is expected first of all to be grown-up. He is expected to have done a lot of reading. He is expected to have a sense of humor. He is expected to pay attention. Those who through stupidity can't meet these expectations, or those who, having different tastes, don't choose to, must find the book unrewarding. This gives them every right to call it 'bad'; because as far as they go, that's just what it is; and their honesty in not pretending that they understood what they couldn't or wouldn't understand is surely commendable

V 26   'Heroic acts' seem as a rule to be more or less involuntary — that is; quite unplanned; done without thinking

V 29   I've always struck myself as a good bit of a son of a bitch; and I can't but feel that anyone who knew as much about me as I knew would share my opinion.

Since everybody does it, dying can't be very hard

the envy, hatred, malice, and all uncharitableness so natural and normal in the creative arts

V 30   to regard the libertine's self-inflicted illnesses as coldly as the military must regard the self-inflicted wound

VI 1   that lost liberalism of disinterested goodwill which perhaps actually existed in a Franklin or a Jefferson. At least, today's self-regard and today's sentimentality never seems to taint their liberalism

VI 7   That a principle pleasure of heaven will be watching the torments of the damned seems plausible when one considers the usual temperament or character of the pious

VI 23   It may be guessed that a good deal of what is taken to be courage is just lack of imagination. The seeming brave man may be too dumb to understand that he is in danger

VI 28   A possible comfort in having no family may be that, as you get older, there'll be no one, or at any rate, only strangers, wishing to God you'd hurry up and die

VI 30   the prickings of dismay in that question which, pausing, pulling up, every mind must from time to time find itself putting to itself: *Who are you?*

VII 1   writer's note: if you find a lot of explaining necessary, something is wrong either with your material or with your approach to it

VII 2   In theological theory, pride may be a deadly sin; but in common practice, pride is responsible for most of what is best in human behaviour

VII 8   The most striking thing about it seemed to me to be the virtually unrelieved imperceptiveness or lack of discernment. Thus handicapped, he probably never knew himself what made him sore. I could tell him. The book was constantly exhibiting a kind of detachment, of observed fact evenly dealt out, no one favored. Nothing is more infuriating to the quasi-liberal, quasi-sentimental mind of almost every 'advanced' or little-magazine critic

VII 13 I started to answer a fellow who wrote saying he could see my books were beautifully and fully planned and how did you go about that. I said I didn't really plan my books and that I doubted if any great book had ever been planned: good books grow on their own. It occurred to me in time that what I really meant was that I don't know how to plan and *my* books just grow

VII 25 That natural wish of the gentle-natured man that the terms of this existence could be so altered that the success, the good fortune, the winnings, of the happy did not have to depend, as they now ultimately do, on the failures, the bad fortunes, the losses, of the unhappy

VII 28 that more or less absolute comparting of life and thought by which the average human being may be, in the course of a day or even of an hour, moved by who knows what, now nearly a saint, now wholly an animal: now so sagacious that you're taken aback; now so stupid that you can hardly believe it

VIII 6   All I know is my hair never used to be grey

VIII 8   A principle of today's liberalism seems to be a bowing and scraping to all minority groups — perhaps because liberals themselves are a minority group. If no sadder, I'm at least wiser in knowing now that if you want to offend (which usually means also, infuriate) a 'liberal' a good way to do it is to treat any minority as though people no different from other people compose it.

VIII 9   While it's no doubt that health comports with temperance alone and you don't get away with dissipation forever, you don't get away with temperance forever, either.

VIII 12   [the M. Schorer MS. Sinclair Lewis An American Life — sent to S]

a sort of appalling interest in such matters as the construction of 'Arrowsmith' with Paul de Kruif. I keep thinking: so this is why everything he did was quite bad. Nobody could work that way and do anything worth reading; but on reflection I'm obliged as always to see what I mean is merely that *I* couldn't; and that when I say his work was quite bad, what I mean is merely that it doesn't interest me.

VIII 30   When Thoreau judged that most men lived lives of quiet desperation I think he failed to consider the fact that, by a merciful provision of Providence, most men have little or no more imagination than an animal. Good reasons for despair may be all around the average man; but he won't see them.*

See Morning Moon and Night, pp. 403-404. Ed.

IX 9   That perplexity of justice in trying to determine how far a man is fairly to be held answerable for having let himself become what he is, and so, more or less unavoidably, does whatever he may have done.

IX 13   The unfortunate fact about 'bias' is that those against whom prejudice is often shown are all too apt, in their pain of wounded feeling, to confirm prejudice's original unfair opinion.

IX 20   "Torquemada's code of instructions (1484) provided that an accused might be tortured if *semiplena probatio* existed against him. i.e. so much evidence as to raise a grave presumption of guilt" Ency Brit V 22 p 311 [The concept of *semiplena probatio*'s great power in shaping every human judgment bears thinking about. Cf. 'vehemently suspected'

IX 21   His finding was the Duc de la Rochefoucauld's: our test of good intelligence is whether or not a man is of our own opinion

X 3   those depressions which are the natural dead-sea fruit of the introspective and imaginative temperament

X 5   He seems to join in about equal parts the bonehead, the sorehead and the solemn ass. You see that some such combination, not just those plain or simple ignorances incidental to it, must have been in Schiller's mind when he wrote the well known line: against stupidity, the gods themselves struggle in vain.

X 6   to anticipate the time when the cat, death, will decide to have some fun with the mouse, me.

At fifteen few boys will have learned either the wisdom or the methods of concealing those elements of the cad and fool which are in all of us

X 7   The reflection that for the first time in history the phenomenon of a great city, like New York, being there in the morning and not being there in the afternoon could perfectly well occur

X 9   [I don't think any experienced writer feels 'pain over a bad review'.* Hostile criticism is much more likely to stir him to a kind of indignation of mind at this asinine expression of what will be bound to seem to him the unfriendly critic's own ignorance and imperception. To be hurt, he'd have to believe his critic was right and this he'll seldom be either willing or able to do. In a throwaway 'Paperback Review' Oct 60 of a few days ago a Terry Southern, noted down as the author of two novels, made some observation on 'the latest style in heroes.' One observation: "On the other hand, a writer of serious pretension or more accurately, one who writes out of some deep personal impulse, consistently strives to create original characters in the manner of, say, Faulkner . . . It is the difference, for example, between Popeye of Sanctuary, an original; and Arthur Winner of By Love Possessed, a copy'. Taking a writer's ordinary umbrage, I'm afraid my reaction (he had pronounced earlier: 'Unhappily the characters and events in a book are almost invariably drawn from the author's *literary* experience rather than from life or from imagination') was: Look, Stupid. It's a copy, all right. That's the whole point in writing fiction for grown-up readers. The copy is from life. Anyone who knows, or moves in, the described circles recognizes him, has seen him. The whole point about created 'original' characters is that no

*This entry begins with a quote from a critic's reply to an author in *The New York Times Book Review*. Ed.

one ever saw them, or ever could see them. They're by definition strictly on paper, and an intelligent reader (as opposed to
literary intellectuals making a cult of the abstract and impres-
sionistic) soon sees there's no reason to waste his reading time
that way. This kind of private sounding-off is surely more often
pleasure than pain [this would also apply, now I think of it, to
the various attacks in Catholic or Jewish pubs. when the book
came out, or in some cases, later, when its supposed 'success'
excited some partisans]

X 10   my writing aim would be not so much to tell the reader new
        things as to remind him of what he knows

X 12   the waiting room of this life, where, with that principle of death
        lurking in you, you must sit until the doctor called your name

X 16   In practice, and for most believers, organized religion is seen to
        be a primitive form of psychiatry

        the ordinary paranoid reaction of projecting hostility on others
        in which the paranoic believes everyone *must* mean to slight or
        hurt him and he'll take care not to be deceived by any appear-
        ances to the contrary

X 19   Once in a while you find someone who so sincerely doesn't give
        a damn about pomp or circumstance, or place or position, that
        he never even bothers to tell you he doesn't give a damn about
        them

X 20   He said his wife was so much younger than he that he must
        expect to predecease her. He wouldn't have a lot to leave; so he
        felt she ought to have some kind of vocational training. As far
        as his time and energy allowed, he had been assiduous about
        seeing she got it; and he flattered himself that even if he died
        tomorrow she'd have no trouble finding work in any whore
        house.

X 21   [concluding part of Mark Schorer MS. on Sinclair Lewis]
        1. George Jean Nathan's alleged comment to SL, who was not
        drinking at the moment, that he was, as a result, "dull, damn
        dull." Other evidence in the good and detailed MS. makes you
        see this might be the case. Most people are certainly seen to
        better advantage sober than drunk, and Lewis was certainly
        average-or-worse awful when drunk: but, poor bastard
        (perhaps because of his skin condition and general appearance)
        he was so self-conscious sober that he was really nastier and
        more tiresome that way than when he'd drunk enough to forget
        his self-consciousness.
        2. His complaint about Williamstown when he had the place
        along our road was that he'd spent a year there and Williams
        College had ignored him (not quite true by the MS. record) and

so to hell with Williams. How far this is a matter of temperament must impress me when I think that I've been pretty close
to his spot for 2 years (come day after tomorrow) and the way
Williams minds its own business fills me with friendly feelings.

X 22 The discomfort, if nothing worse, that a man must generally
feel as he looks back on that son of a bitch, himself when
young.

X 24 He had the usual difficulty in believing that twinge, this trifle of
discomfort, announced the beginning of his end.

X 31 [Selected Letters of Stephen Vincent Benet — Fenton (a damn
bad selector) Yale
In the early part of the book letters to Rosemary Carr (which
she must understandably have cherished and saved) do much to
make you wince. These were of course 'love letters' which are
written to and for one person. Read by anyone else, they're
almost bound to seem silly, affected, coy, and sometimes
maudlin. I suggested to S. that Rosemary, who alone could
have made them available, must be a really dreadful person
(like — vide supra — Sinclair Lewis's wives) with no taste and
no judgment. I'm told no; and I believe it: because reflection
makes you see that no taste and no judgment would be proof
against feeling. The feeling, S. assures me (and indeed there is
plenty of evidence in the letters) was and remained a profound
mutual attachment. With Steve dead, 'Rosemary' could very
well find those saved letters writing of the most moving sort.
They must be printed, not because she wanted people to know
he had been crazy about her, but because she thought (alas!)
they showed how wonderful *he* was.

XI 12 What is called tolerance is in fact a form of indifference. No one
is tolerant where his interests are threatened

XI 16 Copies of a French translation of By Love Possessed (Par
L'Amour Possédé) came today. The translator is a Marie Tadié.
She has a certain amount of the usual French trouble with
English idiom tending to translate literally (which never fails to
surprise me; because next to English, surely French idiom, goes
farthest in laying traps for the literal translator and you'd
expect more wariness): but I was also surprised to find that she
had engaged in a few (I can't but feel) personal trifles of
censorship. The basis of them seems to me astonishing: for I
had always seen the French as commendably free of the nonsense of embarrassment about natural functions. Marie apparently feels that women should not menstruate and did what she
could about suggestions of mine that so they do. I noticed it
because I can still read French with reasonable facility and on p.
33 there was an abrupt transition which didn't sound right to

7

me. Checking it against the English text, I found she'd decided to leave out a paragraph or two which gave sense to that part of the conversational exchange. Thinking carefully, I remembered a couple of the references and checked them. One, in dialogue (p. 131) seemed to defeat her ("depuis quand vous n'avez plus vos régles"): but (p. 174) a box of sanitary napkins becomes a bare 'boîte qui sembla rendre définitive and sans recourse la vérité' etc. This might be a good Gallic touch of not laboring a point (though it is better, whenever you can, to be specific); but one other parenthetical reference (p. 409) was struck out entirely. Since no other (from the prude's standpoint) improper passages were tampered with, I thought this interesting. [I then made a check in eight other translations, which I could figure out, and all of them seemed to follow the text at those points. Very odd]

XI 19 Youth's hunger for admiration and applause, often exacerbated by youth's depressions in self doubt, and in self-knowledge of weaknesses, mistakes, failings to try or to persevere; where what can there be to admire, what to applaud?

She was hurt when she discovered his unfaithfulness with another woman not because she loved him so much but because she loved herself so much

XI 25 [Margaret Culkin Banning sent S. her new book: *Echo Answers*. You can't read far in one of Mrs. B's books without feeling that her mental age is about 14; but while you're feeling that, if you're interested in writing, you may also note that she hasn't written 26 books to no purpose. Such as her material is, she really can handle it. Is there any reason to doubt that fiction more serious and more seriously regarded wouldn't often be the better for some of that old pro. clarity, emphasis, and coherence here conscientiously and expertly devoted to tripe?

XI 29 As I see it, the point isn't: do I like this picture? but: Is this picture true? That isn't the way they see it. In fact how true the picture is may be measured by how mad they are.

XII 6 I had at last to decide (or agree to admit) that my several years' effort on the MS. I had been calling: A Sky-born Music* couldn't by any means be salvaged. That the 16 year old first-person narrator was going to make things hard was I suppose part of the original attraction. The truth now seems to me: if you're truthful; that is, if you write without sentiment and falsification that marks all books about boys that I've ever read, you must show the boy as dull, tiresome and not worth the adult reader's time.

*The opening section of the novel was published as the short story "Eyes to See" in *Children and Others* (New York: Harcourt, Brace & World, 1964). Ed.

XII 7 Jests at scars by those who never felt a wound may be unseemly
and even imprudent: but can it be called unreasonable?

In connection with abandoning ASM the thought came to me
that perhaps the only children an intelligent adult can take
seriously or find interesting are his own children.

XII 12 Elizabeth Taylor's *A Wreath of Roses* has a scene that seems a
fair example of that common writing or rather reading situation in which the author, though the material is all his, doesn't
understand what is going on as well as he has enabled the
reader to. The passage is one that deals with the constraint C.
finds herself feeling with her long-time intimate friend who,
since their last vacationing together has married and had a
baby. Granted that Miss Taylor's Delicacy might forbid her
such thoughts, or at any rate, forbid her writing them down,
the state of C's mind as described of itself suggests the real
reason for the new found ill ease is that C. can't screw up her
courage to ask what she most wants to know about (and which
she could certainly be told about). Both the grossness of the
necessary question and the great loss of face in the question's
admission of an ignorance keep her dumb, make her, in a
frustration of unsatisfied curiosity, pretend unreally that the
matter doesn't interest her. From the dialogue given, the un-
asked, unaskable question doesn't seem to have occurred to the
writer, but it occurs to the reader: viz: "What's it really like?
When you have him in you is it really better? Is the feeling any
different than when you're doing it by yourself?"

[A T. LS photo of Virginia Woolf & her father heading a
review of Woolf's Autobiography made me think she looked
like a book by her [P. FILE]

XII 13 It's said that the years teach patience, that the shorter our time,
the greater our capacity for waiting. I must wonder when this
begins. Not at 57, I know.

Another point of difference in human temperament might lie in
whether the loss of illusions that goes with growing up seems to
you a great pity; or, on the contrary, at least a little something
gained

XII 15 [A title: TIME AND AGAIN

XII 21 *TIME 28/ XII / 60 Letters:* "Time's assurance that the critical
reputation of Norman Mailer has declined [Dec 5 note on M's
stabbing his wife] needs correction. Many critics and fellow
writers feel that Mailers work is of continuing significance and
brilliance etc etc" signed James Baldwin, Jason Epstein, Lillian
Hellman, Alfred Kazin, Robert Lowell, Norman Podhoretz,
Lionel Trilling, William Phillips [This seems interesting as an

indication of just who in 'Literary Circles' determines that shallow, slovenly and phoney writing* is to be treated as Significant and Brilliant — or is there after all some fervid Jewish literary bond? Or is it non-sectarian: merely; what the hell, the guy's in a terrible jam; never mind how he writes?

*the stuff, not of life, but of little-magazine & little 'liberal' college English Course 'literature'. No discerning, reasonably well-read grown up will be interested.

2   24 December 1960-28 June 1961

XII 25   That particular beginning of wisdom which is coming to realize that if you ask too much of yourself you won't get it

the discovery that with the high brow goes as a rule the bone head

the stylized thought and stylized feeling of high-brow criticism

XII 26   To generalize is to simplify. Therefor generalizations can never be true since the truth is never simple

those triumphs of obtuseness in which you find a critic not only missing the author's point but even missing his own point, not seeing the meaning of what he himself is writing . . . that unmistakable cocksureness of self-conceit

XII 29   James Joyce's word games often have real interest and his parodies of style, though too often blurred, can be amusing; but they have nothing to do with 'literature' which, to have any value, has to be some presentation in writing of Milton's new aquist of true experience.

I 16   He seems to be that happiest of men, a really perfect fool. The intelligent, the perceptive, the discerning feel misgivings. They look before they leap. If you exhort them (by the bowels of Christ) to consider could they not be wrong, they will listen. The perfect fool knows no such doubts. His native stupidity, imperceptive, undiscerning, saves him from any self-knowledge, gives him every confidence.

I 16   His work is neither simple nor easy. To appreciate his genius a more than ordinary perception is required. Either you have it; or you don't have it. I don't have it.

I 18   By sentimentality I suppose I mean feeling that is without discrimination because it is without discernment — feeling, perhaps, for feeling's sake. Why this, or its results, should make me recoil, seem to me so wrong & bad, I find a tough question.

I 20   he has been called stupid: but I think he's more foolish or silly than stupid. It's not that he can't think or doesn't know anything. It's that his thinking is always shallow and childish: and an evident imperception, a lack of discernment, limits what he knows of life and men.

I 23   The ordinary eventualities of this existence in which those die who have everything to live for and those survive who have nothing to live for

I 24   Writers may do well to try to avoid clichés: but when they do they often also avoid the clearest, shortest and simplest way of stating their meaning.

I 30   Men aren't so much natural liars as readily suggestible and very subject to mistake

One of those fortunate fools who's stupid enough to be unaware that he's stupid

You must not suppose a thing is impossible just because it's most unlikely

II 10   I can see that, in reason, allowances ought to be made; that, to myself when young, I should be kinder than my inclination now is. Still, it's hard to be reasonable when I recall, as I suppose most of us must, the innumerable injuries done then to present self-regard or self-respect.

II 15   Prof. Perry's op. cit. comment on Mark Hopkins* suggests that the case was what it must almost always be: any man who has great talents or abilities is bound to be part son of a bitch.

*A. L. Perry, *Williamstown and Williams College.* Published by the author, 1904. Ed.

II 20   In fact he had a mind that's all thumbs: confusing ideas, missing points, incapable of making distinctions or thinking anything through. When you first realize it, you may get a shock; but, after all, naturally enough, he is as incompetent in judgment on himself as on every other subject; and though you may be amazed you ought not to be surprised that in his own eyes, he is the most perceptive and discriminating of men

II 20   This morning when I woke up I remember seeing it was December; how, in the space of a day, it can have come, tonight, to be July I don't know, or perhaps fear to think

II 24   Imperception is a man's best friend.

II 26   I'm monarch of all I survey — except of course, myself. Myself's monarch of me.

He said: Pay attention. This is the kind of thing that interests you. Remember?

III 6   Design seems behind much of man's inhumanity to man; but woman's inhumanity to woman often looks like the jealous or miffed impulse of a moment.

III 7   As a rule, what a man loves a woman for is not, as the woman may imagine, her charms of person, but the fact that in thought, word, or deed and often all three she manages consistently to flatter him

III 7   Being sentient, you have to look forward. That's our trouble

III 16   The striking thing about op. cit. above,* which is very good, is how much more rewarding, in terms of that new aquist of Milton's, the book is than anything Joyce ever wrote. The difference I suppose is simply that when you work through Joyce's complications and obscurities you're a little miffed — a second-rate mind has no business to conceal itself that way. It isn't too much and too wise for ordinary clear expression, it's too little and too vapid — the ridiculous or at least exasperating mouse out of the mountain. But Ellmann's mind is first rate; his comment on Joyce's sad and silly times is full of instruction; this is not just from books; this is real and human and fine food for thought.

*Richard Ellmann, *James Joyce* (New York: Oxford University Press, 1959). Ed.

III 18   It would seem to go without saying that those who argue for a change in any social set-up want only changes that would be to their personal advantage. At any rate, you never do hear them say this: all they say is that right and reason, that justice and humanity demand change.

III 19   Having run into real partisan abuse late in my career I'm probably more surprised than I should be to see it has regular tricks or turns. In the English *Books & Bookmen* for March (which is for some reason sent me free) I was glancing through a long rather gabby interview with Monica Dickens, a semi-tripe writer, when my name caught (as only it can) my eye and I learned that in America the influence of the N. Y. Times Book Review had *made* "that dreadful book, By Love Possessed." Which she found a "terrible bore." Remembering a jingle by R.C. light-versifier Phyllis McGinley, sent me a couple of years ago, which had a line about how she 'was awful tired of James Gould Cozzens' I could realize at once that Monica is another more or less pious R.C.
However, a little later, she had occasion to cite me again, pointing out that when I offer "a three page description of the outside of a court house" it is "absolutely unforgiveable" in a

writer. This is a much more interesting phenomenon; and it is general, and must have some general significance. I've never seen a review of hostile intent that didn't have some, and usually, many examples. Here is no mere matter of stupidly misunderstanding or wilfully misrepresenting what was undoubtedly to be found in text on page so and so and which (let us admit) was perhaps not so explicitly stated that you couldn't read it another way if you happened to want to. Neither this nor anything like it is in the text at all. I agree with Monica. To take 3 pages to describe any physical object would seem to me ridiculous. I never did it and never would. The most such a thing ever got from me would be a paragraph and if it wasn't a very short one, it would be because the object's appearance seemed to me to have overtones or implications needed to make some point quite unconnected with the mechanics of bare description. In short, though Monica's sincerity in complaining about it can hardly be questioned, the 'inexcusable' three page description simply isn't there. Now; how or why can she imagine that it was?

IV 13   By listening to what a man says you may or may not learn what he usually thinks; but by watching what he really does you can tell what he really wants. When you know that, you can tell what he thinks.

IV 16   title: A Dream of Avarice

Returning from Communion, he remarked that Our Lord's veins had apparently been filled with cheap California sherry

IV 18   A feeling that a man of Bertrand Russell's intelligence was more likely to be right about the nature of things than a man of Fulton J. Sheen's intelligence.

IV 21   A *Shooting Star* Wallace Stegner's forthcoming novel that Denver Lindley sent me.

on p. 116 is a scene of that interesting (and alas vitiating) kind in which the author shows you that he does not understand his own characters. In the situation he describes the characters he has described wouldn't (any ordinary knowledge of human nature tells you) be doing what he makes them do. Of course it isn't that people *couldn't* do what he says they did; it's that *if* they did it, they could not be as he's displayed and described them. Here, 'Sabrina', you realize, would certainly let her husband sleep with her, regardless of her earlier encounter. He, even if she had said (as the described Sabrina never would) ". . . I'm not fit to . . . oh God, Burke, please. I was with him . . .etc" would, at the stage described, have been much more likely to go right ahead and lay her. As described; he isn't the man on whose 'cheekbone the bed lamp lit the shine of tears' [it would be fair to say more explicitly what as I see it is wrong. I think the author is making his woman attach an unfeminine importance to the sexual act, and more justification or explanation would be needed to make it convincing. I remember a line of Mary McCarthy's: 'When she'd laid it on the line five hundred times, what was one more screw?' Similarly, 'Burke' with her clothes pulled off and 'his face buried in her belly' would be unlikely to quit. If someone else had done it to her, why he'd do it to her, too, the bitch — a form of getting square. [John O'Hara has a passage I think in *From the Terrace* which goes persuasively to this point, even though it's the kind of point O'Hara is far too fond of]

IV 29   What he says is for the most part both stupid and untrue but it goes without saying that he's sincere in every word. Anger is blind, peevishness is imperceptive. It makes you think of the gag: Sure I looked before I turned into the main road. Can I help it if I don't see good?

V 6   It seems true that if you make no point of pursuing Fame, Fame will often turn around and pursue you: but Fame probably runs well only when someone's after it. If it's after you, you needn't be caught unless you want to be; it's easily left behind.

V 9   When this world makes having money so important, so essential to well-being, it's hardly reasonable to blame a man for anything he may have done to try to get himself a supply.

V 14   First of all, how likely is it that a carnivorous mammal like a fox would be jumping to get any grapes, sweet or sour?

V 16   Putnam's sent me *Quest For Innocence* a novel by C. B. Gilford forthcoming. The blurb says: "Mr. G. in treating the complex themes of faith and sin in a suspenseful exciting novel will evoke comparison to some of the leading Catholic novelists of other lands" Mr. G. does indeed 'evoke comparison to' such novelists and the phrasing seems as happy as possible, suggesting exactly that awkwardness of slight artificiality, that indirection of ill-ease that seems to affect fiction defending the faith whenever those 'themes' pop up for treatment. Perhaps this is because a 'Catholic novelist' (like a 'Communist novelist') can't but know he has committed himself to selling something, that he lacks the innocence of purpose, the integrity of disinterest, of the uncommitted novelist who (at least consciously) will have no interest or concern outside reporting life and men as he sees them in a story form with nothing to sell, and so nothing to advertize. This isn't to say that the Catholic 'angle' on the book's action, the Catholic attitudes described are unconvincing. There seems no reason to doubt that this or something like it is how it is in numberless Catholic families:

but the authors themselves (from Evelyn Waugh down) show what the non-Catholic reader can't help feeling are traces of disquiet, some perhaps subconscious awareness of fantasy or even farce in problems of 'sin' which are factitious, not of real life, of the nature of the case, but created by the church's disciplinary rules. It seems very probable that Catholic family conversation can turn on plans being made to shorten time in Purgatory or on deciding which saint would be the better intercessor if you wanted this or hoped to avoid that; but even the Catholic author seems often to be wondering privately if there isn't something crazy in these people and in a morality which eschews evil not because evil is bad in itself — that is, mean or cruel, unbecoming or nasty — but from pure fear of going to hell.

V 18   Some Random Notes for a review of Cordell's Somerset Maugham made before I decided I couldn't do it (for Buckley's *National Review*)

— that the generation of literary criticism by which Maugham has been neglected has been in its pronouncements so nonsensical and imperceptive that the neglect might be said to honor him.

an age of critical aberration which is perhaps best exemplified in such phenomena as a solemnly named '[James] Joyce Scholarship'

Why the more solemn and self-important forms of criticism, the critics called by the late Bernard De Voto Deckle Edged, passed him over is plain. Maugham's writing, lucid and explicit, provides no material for their nonsense. In the up-sidedown world of fashionable letters M's virtues become positive vices

A writer should never come right out and say what he means. This is to be guilty of competence. If you're going to be Great you must leave things uncertain, barely hint at this, vaguely suggest that, offer proper latitude for long speculation on what you really meant

The only thing fiction can have to offer an intelligent adult is Milton's new acquist of true experience. Such an acquist may of course be offered in different ways. Passages may even be found in the writings of such contemporaries of M's as Virginia Woolf and D. H. Lawrence which convey it, or more often, almost convey it.

The manner is valued for its own sake, not for its matter, which, when disentangled, is apt to be found either untrue, or if true, true as a truism is true, giving you no information of use or interest

to illuminate the reader's own experience, not to press on him the experiences of the writer

The thing most held against Maugham is obviously the fact that he made critics and criticism unnecessary. He never wrote a line that needed to be explained (or explained away) No 'interpretation' was required. Any adult reader takes his meanings at a glance: he writes to be instantly understood. The literary rubbish of symbolism, of 'levels of meaning' is never allowed to clutter up his prose or obscure his thought

One aspect of their criticism is that sort of distinctive imperceptiveness, that seeming almost-total ignorance of human beings, human nature, human life that the communist announces in the fact that he can accept communism: and indeed the number of these critics who are (or were when it was perfectly safe to be) party-liners or fellow travelers is suggestive.

V 19   *Having it Both Ways at Once*
What shapes you is not the run of ordinary experiences, it's the experience out of the ordinary. Those are the moments you remember. On the other hand, what shapes you is what you do every day. You may remember better what is different; but what you are will always be what you don't remember.

V 27   It's a melancholy fact of our human nature that not many of us, faced with what we think is an opportunity to show ourselves off as a little better or higher, physically, mentally, morally, or socially than in fact we are, succeed in resisting the temptation.

Sentimentality is often seen as a fault of kindness, of the soft or warm heart. That is just what it isn't. Sentimentality is basically insensitiveness, undiscerning and imperceptive. When you discover that someone is a sentimentalist, look for him to be stupid, dishonest and cruel too.

VI 6   Distinguishing between stupidity and the ignorance of inexperience is often hard because their immediate results are the same. Yet they should not be confused. Ignorance and inexperience are both curable. If it is from either of them that a person's mistakes proceed, and you are sure it is, he should be given another chance. Stupidity on the other hand is incurable. A person who is seen to be plain stupid shouldn't be given another chance.

VI 9   I suppose you ought to remember that when someone turns the talk to let you know he is pretty important, he pays you the compliment of indicating that your respect and admiration would be worth something to him.

VI 12   the often observed fact that the man who is moved to denounce faults in others will generally be loudest in denouncing not the faults that may in fact be theirs but faults of his own which he ascribes to them

VI 13   *A Thing of the Past*

VI 28   In connection with unfavorable comment in *Time* on John Steinbeck's new book* (in fact, it is mawkish and bad: I could not get thru the copy DL sent me) I remembered that he is one of those writers who say they never read reviews: and how I used to think, and indeed state, that they were unwise: that unfavorable criticism, at least, ought always to be read. At that time no book of mine had ever had the kind of 'success' (sales must be in the hundred thousands) that attracts real attention: so to put it as gently as possible I didn't know what I was talking about. Obviously the non-readers know what I have since learned. Such 'success' has to mean that a good deal of the criticism subsequent will consist not in worthwhile analysis of those faults no book can be without and which you'd do well to ponder; but in stupid or partisan personal abuse, the attacks of disguised envy and malice. Reading any of it's a silly waste of time: there'll be nothing there worth serious consideration

The Winter of Our Discontent (New York: Viking, 1961). Ed.

3   3 July 1961-17 January 1962

VII 3   The chronic little-mag. complaint that creative writers are not regarded and respected in materialistic America seemed pretty well answered by the radio and newspaper reception of intelligence that Ernest Hemingway, whether by design, or as the not very convincing suggestion was, by accident, had shot himself to death yesterday morning. It was true it was a Monday and the day before a holiday (supposing design; you might wonder if Mr. H, never one to shun publicity, took it into account) and news would be in short supply: but anyway it was a good big front page story in the Times and Herald Trib and the Wall Street Journal's severely boiled down column of news even had a several line paragraph at the bottom. Certainly no business magnate or industrial leader would have got anything like the space. (The same refuting situation may perhaps be seen in Who's Who, where almost any two-bit writer is sure to be listed, while men of large affairs and really important economic power will be passed over by the hundreds)

[Reflecting on Mr. H's work, about which 20 or 30 literary figures collected by the Times properly said nothing if not good, I found I was indecently disinclined to change my opinion that it always had been and was still too bad so indisputable a talent for writing should have had to go with thinking so callow and childish and feeling so often cheap and silly.

VII 5   In judging character, most of us, untaught by experience, persist in what could be called a fallacy of entities. For the honest man to steal, for the kind man to be cruel, for the brave man to be cowardly (and, indeed, for the bad man to be good) in this fallacy is out of character, and so out of the question. The great truth about character is that no such entities as the honest man or the bad man exist: there are only men: and in never learning, or in forgetting, this is the root of all misjudgment.

VII 13   To communicate as clearly as possible what experience has meant to me

VII 15   *Note on a 'Liberal'.* What repells and annoys me is not his 'liberal' views — most of my own views are if anything more 'liberal' than his. It is the never-absent bonehead presumption with which he hands down on what, you see in a minute, he has neither the experience or the intelligence to understand; the all-sided obtuseness, the basically sentimental lack of discernment or discrimination which always leads him to love dearly the phoney, the unreal, the not-thought-out, the condition contrary to fact. Perhaps intuitively he sees that if these prevailed, were *the* standards, he would be quite important and powerful. While, as it is . . .

VII 19-
VII 22   *By Love Possessed* was opening at the Capitol: and though I thought little of the idea, at loose ends after lunch at the Harvard Club I followed S's suggestion and went up. I must admit I got several surprises. For one thing, the photography was simply and even, sometimes, amazingly, beautiful. For another, the direction gave constant signs of intelligence, especially in small touches, often faithfully taken from the book. When law, for instance, was touched on the to-be-expected nonsense was carefully not made of it. The simplification, by sometimes telescoping, sometimes eliminating characters obviously necessary if the material was to be got into any actable form, showed evident judgment. Flabbergasted, I can only say that, taken all in all, I found it a good deal better than the critics (who probably missed all the good careful small points) claiming it made a mess of the book, had allowed.

VII 29   *TLS VI 14 Middle* comment of Richard Cordell's Maugham
"... *Cakes and Ale* which is so successful in its peripheral

ironies, shows in dealing with human relationships one of those
touches of vulgarity that are so damaging to Mr. M's stature as
an artist . . . On the night of her child's death she went out etc
and returned home on the following morning 'You've come
just in time' her husband says 'I was going to eat your sausage'.
The scene has a 'shocking' effectiveness of the most garish
theatrical kind and so has the actual line that ends the book
when Rosie asked why she ran away with . . . George Kemp
looks at a photograph . . . 'like a publican dressed up in his best
to go to the Derby' and says 'He was always such a perfect
gentleman.' How could any serious novelist attribute to a great
writer (and Driffield whether or not he was modelled on Hardy
is supposed to have been a great writer) a scene of such vulgarity as the climax to a book: worse still, how could a serious
novelist end his own book with such a bit of pinchbeck irony?
Think of Flaubert, James, Turgenev, even Maupassant, and
one has to descend a long ladder to reach Mr. Maugham."
[Words almost fail you. The right question seems to be: How
could any serious critic be such an imperceptive bonehead?
Ans. He couldn't. Exactly what this one means by 'vulgarity'
isn't clear; but if it may be taken as a tendency toward the false,
the cheap, the silly, everyone of the writers named gives you a
good deal of it while M. never gives you any. In the instances
cited, the suggestion that the effectiveness is 'of the most garish
theatrical kind' could come only from someone who was capable of being 'shocked' by the simple and natural (likely; if he
sees his mentioned writers as at the top of that 'long ladder').
To see either as vulgar you'd surely have to be yourself a
humorless, undiscerning and natural born vulgarian and so
always afraid of being exposed for what he knows he is. To
anyone with adult knowledge of life and men both lines must
ring true and if this self-conscious dainty taste finds 'vulgarity',
it is, all ignorant of the obvious truth, finding it in life, not in
Maugham. In short, Maugham's great failings in our literary
age of 'James Joyce Scholarship' clearly come of undue care for
simplicity, clarity, and truthfulness in what he writes.

VIII 3   A point at which just staying alive took all his time and all his
strength. With none of either to spare he could no more work
than he could play.

he had always been less interested in what people thought of
him than in what he thought of them

VIII 6   *Note on Established Reputation* Schachner's seemingly well-
document *Aaron Burr* can leave no doubt at all that in his
relations with Jefferson and Hamilton, Burr was the man of
honor, while the other two were cheats, contemptible sneaks
and malicious liars.

VIII 8   *The Actual Facts of A Matter*
In Chicago, one no doubt wintry night a week or so before
Christmas, 1902, after my mother and father had gone to bed,
my father, very likely a little shy about what both seem to have
regarded as the indecency involved, but feeling perhaps a need
for physical relief, offered probably in silence, to have sexual
connection with my mother. Without pleasure (she told me she
never had pleasure in coitus) but with the perfect readiness of
her wish to have a child (not to be doubted for she had been
consulting a physician about why she hadn't had one) my
mother acquiesced. Their notion of refinement would make it
unlikely that either removed night clothes or uncovered anything not necessary to uncover. These modest adjustments
made my father, placing himself above her and between her
parted legs, presented to the labia the prepuce of his erect penis.
After some thrusts with it to part them, he was able to force his
organ fully into her vagina. The timing in terms of the interval
between the menses, happened to be right. Ovulation had
taken place: and from the gobbet of semen presently ejaculated
by my father against the cervix of my mother's uterus, one
spermatozoon swam its way up, found the ovum: and that was
the beginning of me.*

*See *Morning Noon and Night* (New York: Harcourt, Brace & World, 1968),
pp. 6-8. Ed.

VIII 10   The point about modern medical science keeping people alive
so long after they would normally have died: one gain. More
and more funerals, instead of being occasions for grief, are
happy occasions, relieving and cheering all the next of kin.

VIII 24   Somerset Maugham has pointed out that a writer who studies
to avoid clichés isn't always well-advised. Many of them have
gained through prolonged use an idiomatic value, and in de-
vising other phrasings to substitute for them you will often
sacrifice both precise meaning and effective expression.

VIII 30   *Henry Miller. Tropic of Cancer* The great trouble is that the
book must seem tiresome to any adult reader who keeps up
with 'modern' writing because he's read it all so many times
before. Of course, this is not Mr. Miller's fault. If censorship
hadn't prevented American publication when it was written,
the reader would find he'd read it a good many fewer times than
the case is today. However, it occurs to me that it is so praised
by Advanced Critics for just that reason. It contains exactly
(and all) the stuff that a Work of Genius, by their decree, must
contain. In short, both manner and material are straight Modern Hysterical; and the one noticeable innovation seems to be
the surely minor one of incessant reference to women as cunts.
This bold stroke serves, at least, as perhaps timely reminder

that the work, and the rest of the coterie literature like it, really addresses itself to the young — or, better, the non-adult, who can still be shocked and still find being shocked an exciting literary experience. Seen this way, the persistence of what might be called (in Mr. Miller's own language) the Fuck Everything School is easier to understand.

IX 2   A melancholy fact of the human condition is that most men can come to know what they ought not to do only through having done it.

There is a fiction that people who do unwise or wrong things usually justify what they do by some line of reasoning that makes their acts right. I wonder if this is ever true except perhaps among the wholly unbalanced. Average behaviour suggests that they're perfectly aware of the unwisdom or the wrong and wish they didn't have to do it but interest or appetite leaves them no alternative

IX 4   That nothing succeeds like success may sometimes be true; what's always true is than nothing offends like success

IX 19   The *Living Church* notes that Presiding Bishop Lichtenberger remarked of the 15 clergy who got themselves arrested in Jackson Miss. 'for attempting to use interstate facilities' that they were 'brave men who are acting in a very courageous way.' I'm inclined (I suppose by youthful conditioning) to guess this view may be the right one, yet my moral obtuseness (I speak seriously) is such that I can't see them as either very brave (what were they risking? An arrest & fine, with a fair assurance that publicity they got would take care of both) or very good. I think a man may indeed have a moral obligation to do what he believes is right; and perhaps particularly when doing it involves practical considerations of good sense and expediency, since how else can he enjoy the gratifications of confirmed self-righteousness that he seems to have decided are his greatest good? But, unless this practical consideration is overriding; what obligation to be respected has he to busy himself with efforts to change, correct or improve beliefs of other people, thus bringing them to join him in that wisdom and virtue that he knows to be his?

IX 21   I was looking at Henry James' *Daisy Miller* (of course, because I thought I remembered a point made that I might want to find a way to make). I could not find it, perhaps because my memory was some forty years old. Critically, it was respected then and still, at least in the little mags., seems to be. But what I was struck by was the obvious truth that nobody, simply reading as an adult reader, not knowing it was respected and 'ought' to be read, would be likely to read beyond the first few pages.

IX 24   Putting away some file folders of BLP stuff a number of letters
reminded me of what I'd pretty well forgotten — the real fury of
the attacks on it & me which the book's 'success' had provoked, and how ingenuously unprepared for it I had been. As
long as what I wrote was read only by the handful of literate
(not literary) grown-ups it was written for I was, you'd gather,
unobjectionable. But when, by one of those accidents of publishing, about as impossible to pre-arrange as hitting a slot-
machine's jackpot, everyone was brought to read or try to read
a book of mine, a slowly growing howl went up. Much like the
machine's sudden avalanche of nickles, and evidently triggered
by it, a sudden down-pour of partisan abuse began, much of it
personal (not real literary criticism), all of it blind, and some of
it crazy. Though I'd read about this kind of thing, and how you
must expect it, I suppose I couldn't have quite believed those
sound advices. It is true that I'd thought very often that other
writers' books that were selling a lot were of little merit, and
didn't hesitate to say so; and since tastes differ, I could well
believe the same might be thought and said about me. The
active animus that had to go further I wasn't capable (no doubt
through indifference) of feeling, so I seem to have doubted that
anyone else really felt it.

IX 26   An amusing thing to be noticed in Henry James' *'Short Novels'*
is the acerb little note, struck again and again, of what seems
clearly Novelist's Revenge. From it you can't but suspect that in
English Social Life J. had fairly often been made to feel his
incurable inferiority as an American. But in his fiction, standards of London society are not quite, quite, compared to those
of New York: and compared to an American gent, English
baronets will as often as not be of inferior breeding.

IX 27   *TIME letters* (in connection with my IX 24 note): one Paul W.
Ferris, on the recent 'cover piece' on J. D. Salinger, makes a
point: "It will now be fascinating — in a morbid and unrewarding way — to watch the hatchet men of academe attempt
to prove that no writer earning a Time cover story can possibly
be of literary consequence. Those same precious people who
nibbled at James Gould Cozzens will be quoting paragraphs
out of context, accusing Salinger of writing like Salinger, reading in their own Freudian fantasies etc" [For some reason I
hadn't given much weight to that. Hell, you might say: *Time*
has someone on the cover every week: but of course it's true
they only have about one writer a year: and, now I think of it,
the more crazily abusive critics were always digging out, in my
case, hunks of the incredible TIME Crap they seemed to have
been able to swallow; and so, in short, the 'success' of the
'cover story' may indeed be what they can't take; not, mere
best-selling, or diffused illiberal opinion.

X 4   He said: Sir, I can see that your opinion on this point is interesting to you; but what can be making you imagine it's interesting to me?

X 13   A probably important principle in polemics is not to waste your time charging a man with his real faults. If his faults are real, they'll always speak for themselves. What you should do is note carefully any undeniable merits he has, and state flatly that he lacks them. This is practicable because those who know his merits aren't going to listen to you anyway: while those who don't know them will tend to believe you (the always sound tactic of the Big Lie) and so may be kept from ever discovering the truth.

X 14   Henry James *Lady Barberina*. The strong sense of unreality J. conveys here is a most interesting example of the effects of convention of his day (and perhaps of his nature) that forbade any mention of sexual matters. It might be argued that, since any experienced adult would understand it, there is no need to make the point that Lady B., if she were sexually awakened and being satisfied by the doctor, would be perfectly happy in New York (or anywhere else) and indeed in his foil of Lady A as much as is suggested (though I'm not sure J. knew what he was suggesting). The result is a presentation with precision and discernment of a lot of piffle, since the heart of the matter — how the copulating was going — can only be alluded to in the final note (so wonderful in its phrasing that, having got the doctor to take her back to England, she 'presented him with a little girl.'

X 17   Any young man who, hopeful, believes the dictum of that scurrilous versifier about 'women will have it if 'tis to be had' is going to get quite a surprise when he approaches actual women in real life.

My only weapon is my tongue; so anyone who refuses to listen to me has me licked.

X 23   The great use of a sense of humor is the sharp eye it gains you for the absurd. This means that, other things being equal, you'll make a fool of yourself a good deal less often than the humorless man.

X 29   *H. James Mme. de M. p. 11** "Even after experience had given her a hundred rude hints, she found it easier to believe in fables when they had a certain nobleness of meaning than in well attested but sordid facts."
[Though this describes recognizably and well an often observed state of emotional affairs, are the terms quite right? Do

*"Madame de Mauves." Ed.

'fables' ever prevail when facts are in fact 'well attested' from the standpoint of the believer in them? The truth surely could be that 'fables' are believed in only because imperception or wishful thinking makes *them* seem 'well attested' facts.

XI 4   It would be a strange writer who didn't think it hard that some books should sell a lot, but not his.

XI 8   Death's intolerable invasion of privacy

XI 15   The scenes of my childhood (and indeed, youth, and young manhood), when fond recollection restores them to view, I must admit I don't like at all. Most of them make me ejaculate silently: Oh, dear; oh God: or oh Hell. As a rule, you will be closest to the truth if you assume you're no different than everyone else: but here, I wonder. A slightly psychopathic self-conscious, which doesn't need to be general, often seems suggested when I find myself remembering this or that and saying: 'Ah; you son of a bitch!' Why not just forget it? Could it be a subconscious fear that though (or even because) you may have done relatively all right later it may always come out that you really aren't much good, if the truth were known; now, any more than then?
        [but on the whole, I guess it is just a symptom of what theologians call the Sin of Pride: you think so well of yourself that you feel you should have done better than you know you did.

XI 17   He's entitled to his opinions. They don't sound very intelligent; but, what the hell, being stupid's not against any religion.

XI 20   It was a bad day for contemporary letters when the first myth was invented.

XI 23   The habit of dispassionate and disinterested thinking is surely a good one; yet it may have drawbacks when a man is attacked. The charges against him can be absurd, evident nonsense, demonstrable untruth: but who is so judging them? Why, he is! And are not these the findings that suit him best? They are. And a man, you hold, should be judge in his own case?

XI 26   John O'Hara's new book of short pieces* seems to be being reviewed with a kind of relief, as though the critics feared a new novel. I can understand. The last three or four very long novels have been, essentially, the same book done over and over about the same unnaturally (at least in print) mean, ugly-mooded and stupid people. Yet it is also a fact that there is not a single contemporary writer I've read over the years who has left me, as a kind of residue of the reading, anything like so many well-remembered lines, tags, and bits of dialogue and description that come often to mind.

Assembly (New York: Random House, 1961). Ed.

XII 3   Ed Newhouse, who is good, shrewd and accurate in relating things about people, gave some examples of things done to hurt and humiliate other people by those who happened to have the power to do it. Pondering the point, I had to see that this seemed to be usually an impulse to torment the weak. It occurred to me that the impulse to torment might not be absent in me — but, fun, if I found it that way, would have to be, for whatever psychopathic reason, in offering to torment the strong. The stern joy, I suppose, that ill-tempered warriors feel in foemen they take to be worth licking

The high farce of half-wit impudence pointing with pride, now solemn, now angry, to its own stupidities, ignorances, and imperceptions.

XII 13   He said: To 'celebrate' Christmas a man must be mad. The day should be nothing but one of mourning. That birth — or, since there is no sufficient evidence that it ever actually occurred, let us say, the persuasion that it did — has incontestably been the cause of more human woe, more bestial behaviour, more stupidity and more active suffering than any one other factor in the last 2000 years of history.

XII 17   He didn't lack the will to be devious, only the skill

XII 22   Query to the *Times Lit. Sup.*: Just how does an anonymous letter, which is everywhere treated with contempt, differ from an unsigned review?

I began writing long before I'd had enough experience to know truths of life from untruths so my first books weren't and aren't worth any intelligent adult's attention.

XII 24   *WMNB* put on late this afternoon the tape recording of a reading of what seemed to be the whole text of Dickens' *Christmas Carol*. It was of course inflicted on me as a child when I doubt if I minded much; though later I was able to form a vague impression that it was pretty bad. But until this afternoon, making myself listen with a kind of horror, I had certainly given it less than its due as the crowning achievement of our letters in unadulterated cheap and false feeling. That millions listen to it every year without throwing-up seems to say something pretty sobering about our times.

XII 25   The morning papers reported that Robert Hillyer, 65, admitted to a Wilmington Delaware hospital Saturday died yesterday of a heart attack. The obituary in the NY Times was good & long and Robert would have liked it. [In part this is what I've come to recognize as what might be called Pulitzer-Prize-treatment. If you've won one, the newspapers, or their morgues, adopt you and you get newspaper space in the same way that newspaper men who die, even if nobody ever heard of them, are sure of at least some newspaper space]. I'd gather that Robert was taken by surprise, since an address in the new Kent Alumni Directory indicated he had planned to go to the Virgin Islands this winter and stay there. Getting old myself I can see it as a kind of sudden cutting-off (a man of twenty would surely laugh) before his time, appropriate enough in a life story of minor triumphs and not so minor but somehow muted, disasters; and the thought, I'm afraid, came to me that now if I wanted I could write about it.

XII 27   *Old Lover's Lament.* As she spoke of her marriage's early years, of how happy these were, he had been shocked a little by her expression, strange, even a little ugly on an aging face, of what he had to see was sensuality. Yet, was a person any less bereft, less forlorn, because the fled comforts might have been gross, the help that failed only one-time prowess at easing a between-the-forks itch? Why would sorrow be more creditable if it happened to be for lost and gone days of companionship, for the cups of kindness, the accustomed sharings, that went into 'living together'; or for intimacies whose unenthusiastic decency could be summed up in 'sleeping together'. Coming to mind here, wringing her so hard with loss's pain, was something both less and more than those general phrasings. Desperately, indecently, she here recalled nothing less that the actual one-time knowings of her by man. Familiar heat's specific moments were reviewed. She remembered those early years of nights; of how it had been when together they lay naked and embraced to begin, while slow kissings stirred anticipation's depths: and, in progressive eager pushes, what-you-never-named came rising past her (also unnamed) soft ruff of secret hair, climbing quarter-inch by quarter-inch against the curved soft abdomen above; growing readier and readier for the great good work, joy of heaven to earth brought down, when, her table spread, her come-and-get-it signalled; oh then! oh then! oh then! Yes; then! But now, no more. All over now. All passion, all possibilities of passion, spent a great while since, a long, long time ago. [The difficulties of conveying true sexual experience would seem to remain

XII 30   It is possible to doubt that love's roots are always in selfishness? Love's abnegations, sacrifices, layings down of life (this is spoken of: but is it in fact ever done?) are feeling's chosen treats. Layers of more or less handsome cant may cover them: but underneath are they ever anything more or less heroic efforts to make one's own emotional lot more agreeable, to pull out the kind of plum that lets you say: what a good boy am I?

XII 31   In practice certain obscurities of style, though they may repel many readers, can and do serve the reputation of several authors very well. They make certain that no one is going to see right away how banal the material is, or how childish or second rate the thinking. And this is not the end. Hardly anyone who has put himself to the long trouble of guessing meanings so hard to get at is going to admit that the findings weren't worth the work — or, bluntly he has let himself be made a fool of. He will in nine cases out of ten save face by being next to the author himself in claiming this work is of Profound Significance.

I 1   OTC.* *Mary McCarthy*'s literary pieces offer the perhaps amusing suggestion that though she got rid of Edmund Wilson as a husband she never got rid of his critical opinions and repeats them with an unreasoned awe though sometimes they don't sort too well with her native critical common sense and sound taste.

On The Contrary (New York: Farrar, Straus & Cudahy, 1961). Ed.

I 6   In connection with MM's echoes of Edmund Wilson (I/1 supra) I was pondering the not too relevant point of just why I disagreed with them, of why I find *War & Peace* and the Russian novels in general, and indeed a number of other masterpieces by common high brow consent, uninteresting and unreadable. It seems to come down to what is for me the utter impossibility of accepting or believing in their characters. In the case of *War & Peace*, for instance, I'm quite prepared to learn that Russian attitudes of mind, Russian feeling, talk, and action, may differ from anything I have seen: yet to be acceptable the account of these differences must limit or confine them to the practicable. People may indeed behave very oddly; but when they do, the writer presenting them must do it with an explanatory insight that makes me see how and why. When I'm given a mere flat announcement that this was said, done, or thought when in my experience it wouldn't have been, I balk. I feel very much as I would if my author asked me to believe that certain people, by waving their arms, can fly like birds. True, I've never met any of the people he speaks of, nor been where he says they live; but my general experience is ample to make me certain that no people anywhere can do any such thing. The writer who persists in such representation is a liar or a fool: and I have no more time for him.

As you grow old, years may get shorter and shorter: but moments can be just as long as ever

I 13   *The Search for 'Bias'.* The fact that you might not be able to show real grounds for calling the attitude 'prejudiced' didn't mean that you couldn't, by reading a certain way — the way made easy by your own self-conscious oversensitiveness — read into it something you could and would find more infuriating than mere open hostility. This would be some imagined calm of disdain, galling in its very absence of animus, in what might even be its quiet overtones of regret to have to acknowledge that these people (you) are (let us face it!) rather unlikeable, just won't do; and might as well be dismissed.

4   18 January 1962-20 July 1962

I 18   A note of falseness in the 'liberal' stereotype of fiction (and often of reports supposed to be factual) that is sure to show the man in authority careless about the poor and weak but zealous to please the rich and strong. Perhaps there was a time when this might have been true; but under today's conditions, the man who gets authority is much more likely to let the poor and weak have every break. Obviously nothing else would so titillate the pleasure of powers he must have craved when he struggled for his position. On the other hand, today's rich and strong aren't that rich and strong. He can safely, and so he is likely to, throw the book at them just to let them know he's not as no-account as he may think his position makes them suppose him.

I 20   The pet name he kept for that long-lost person, himself when young was an unsmiling: *You Son of a Bitch!* A hundred, perhaps a thousand, specific recollections, visiting him in vacant or in pensive mood, flashing on that inward eye could make him pull-up, silently forming the phrase in his mind while in deepest self-dislike he asked (and in vain): how could you ever have said that, how could you ever have done that? To be sure, one (though seemingly not he) might argue that he exaggerated; that he was unduly, improperly hard on that person. Practically all the wounding recollections were of awkwardnesses, stupidities, more or less trivial and momentary meannesses, trifling lies or breaches of faith. What they weighed on, he had to see, was his conceit, not his conscience. They lacked even the dignity of consequence that true crime might have. That is; failing at goodness, he could also be said to have failed at badness; as a villain, never really amounting to anything; never achieving any status higher than that of unsavory, or at most, contemptible, character.

I 30   The material* brought several of the English notices on the

*The entry begins with a comment on the style of Richard Hughes's *The Fox in the Attic* with a list of examples of what Cozzens described as "lapsing into whimsy, now arch, now coy, now verbally crooking the little finger".

jacket blurb to mention Tolstoy (along with genius). What
seemed an odd coincidence when Augustine got to Germany
that unhappy mingling of fictional characters and historical
persons began in the very worst manner of *War & Peace* which
was plainly being copied in a small way. I don't mean it was any
worse here than there, merely that I find it bad and tedious
everywhere.
[In short, this seems to be the kind of writing (my own is
another) that must have some emotion-arousing quality that
makes those who like it unable to see its faults; and those who
don't like it, unable to see its merits. The result is no critical
middle ground. The likers, in effect, love it and give it the
highest praise: the dislikers are not just bored or indifferent. In
effect, they hate it; actively and loudly they assert it's as bad as
possible.

II 1   It's to be noticed that the balderdash about money not buying
happiness comes from those who know nothing about it because they have little money. No rich man ever finds sincere
fault with money or honestly wishes he were without it. Verb.
sap.?

II 4   *Schorer: Lewis p. 355* quoting Harold Stearns. "These contentions are exactly the contentions of Babbit. The first is that in
our business civilization we are hypocrites, that there is an
appalling gap between our profession and our practice. . . . the
most moving and pathetic fact in the social life of American
today [is] our emotional and aesthetic starvation . . . [Schorer
concludes] . . . a culture that was just becoming aware that it
could not tolerate what it had made of itself."
[Clearly critics' talk. Who but more or less high brow critics
ever found that gap 'appalling'? 'Business civilization' you can
be sure always took such a fact of human nature in its stride.
The critics may be starving, but there's no indication that
people, in the main, weren't getting as much as they wanted of
what they liked; and it seems safe to say that what the culture
'had made of itself' was by everyone but those critics, not only
tolerated, but warmly embraced.

II 5   In connection with the critical attitude above one should
perhaps ponder two observable facts about literary criticism as
practised. As a rule, reviews are much too kind. It seems
impossible to write a book so bad that quite a few reviewers
won't say it's good. It seems equally impossible to write a book
so good that partisan feeling won't say, often with fury, that it's
very bad.

II 6   The observable truth seems to be that almost all failures are
demonstrable just deserts; brought about by stupidity or incapacity; earned and meritted. On the other hand, successes,

just as observably, don't have to be deserved. Like the rain, they fall on the just and the unjust. You don't have to be intelligent, or industrious, or good: you only have to be a certain man at a certain place at a certain time. In short; failure is seldom just bad luck; while success may very well be just good luck.

II 7   There's surely irony of some delicate, ultimate sort in the fact that a long biographical and critical study may present the material so intelligently and so lucidly that it makes a great deal more rewarding, more thought-provoking, reading than anything the writer written about ever wrote. This has been some twice recently. (Ellmann's *Joyce*: Schorer's *Lewis*).

II 8   *Why silence is golden.* The just complaint must always amount to a self-serving declaration: and the juster, the more cogent or reasonable, the complaint, the worse for you. Your obvious anxiety to do right by yourself can never be engaging. What complaint gets you is just the opposite of what you're making it in the hope of getting. With every word, you're not winning, you're alienating the average person's sympathies.

II 9   There are no new 'truths'; all truths are old and worn: so if it's true it won't be new, and if it's new it won't be true.

II 11   An image of the state of the world. In a sinking boat, the people packed together are engaged in a brawl, actually, a battle-royal. Every man for himself, the fighting maniacs clubbed and stabbed and shot each other, regardless of the inflow of water mounting around their knees.

II 12   What you learn from it is that no matter how hard he tries or how careful he is a writer can't make his work fool-proof. The fool will cut you down to his size and there's nothing you can do about it.

II 13   The everyday comedy — or perhaps, rather, farce — of the perfect fool who, certain he is the wisest of men, pontificates unabashed.

II 17   *D. Macdonald Anthology of Parodies**
This Random House collection, or at least the idea of it, was very puzzling. Having seen a demonstration of the editor's absolute humorlessness and nearly total imperceptiveness this would be the last job in the world I'd expect him to take on. His own offers at wit are always so embarrassingly awful you wouldn't expect him to understand or be able to relish the subtle wit of a really good parody. Explanation through examination. He does neither. Though large enough to include some very good parodies, the selection is altogether undiscriminating and so lets you guess the truth. Parodies appeal to

Parodies, ed. Dwight Macdonald (New York: Modern Library, 1960). Ed.

him not because they can be very funny (he wouldn't know about that) but because he sees them as what he *does* relish; exercises in scorn, malice, and derision meant to pain the persons parodied. You can make the further guess that, like many people with no sense of humor, he is personally hyper-sensitive to criticism, able to see nothing absurd about himself. Represented as absurd, others too, he could angrily hope, might cry with his kind of vexation: and *that* would be for him!

III 2   He had to see that the operation of Fortune, in delivering him from encounters with those parts of human nature which are envy, hatred and malice, and all uncharitableness, in throwing him almost altogether with people fair in statement, reasonable in judgment, and honest in motive, might not, in the end, prove fortunate. In effect, he was deprived of a forewarning which would have let him do a little fore-arming.

III 27   The meek, apologetic, almost supplicating, expression common to men self-defeated — the compulsive drinker; the chronic failure in business: the man whose troubles are his own fault and who unhappily knows them to be.

III 28   A surprising conclusion experience forces on you: what scientific demonstration has proved false may often remain true as a matter of the observable facts of life.
         ... How much that has been shown to be without scientific foundation remains as a matter of observable fact true.

IV 6   An engraved card came yesterday reading: *The President & Mrs Kennedy request the pleasure of the company of Mr and Mrs Cozzens at dinner on Sunday April 29, 1962 at eight o'clock.* Attached was a Black Tie card; White House gate pass; and a card saying let the Social Secretary know. I of course let her know at once that would she thank the President & Mrs K but we regretted we couldn't be in Washington that day. My policy of having no dinner jacket seemed to pay off (could any such occasion be worth what it would cost to have Brooks make me up one in a hurry?) but I still felt a certain discomfort — if they, or most likely, 'Jackie', were trying to be nice to the Creative Arts, was it kind to kick the bumbling effort in the teeth? Not that I was going to change my mind: but I was amused to realize what relief (and, perhaps, subconscious offence, which worked the relief?) I felt when S. today found a *NY Times* story that said 150 people were invited to that Sunday night dinner to 'honor' Nobel Prize winners. Or, in short, the President & Mrs K. were probably going to be pleased to hear from The Social Secretary that at least a few of those invited would be helping to thin the crowd by not coming.

IV 7   a trick of style which, with elaborate wordings, created the fancy image through a paragraph and finished by dealing it a cut, the more brutal for being so casual, across its false face.

IV 10   By a merciful provision of Providence, youth, like death is something that can only happen to you once.

IV 12   Aldous Huxley's *Island* and Katherine Anne Porter's *Ship of Fools* are rather depressing in their suggestion that a compulsory retirement age for writers might be a good idea. Miss Porter's 'long-awaited' work has an introductory note: "The title of this book is a translation from the German etc . . . I read it in Basel in the summer of 1932 etc . . . I took for my own this simple almost universal image of the ship of this world on its voyage to eternity. It is by no means new — it was very old and durable and clearly familiar when Brant used it; and it suits my purpose exactly. I am a passenger on that ship. K.A.P."
[You have been warned; and no kidding. *Time* 'The art is consummate'
Huxley, while never so pretentious or inane, has for 'characters' a set of preaching puppets he wouldn't have tolerated for a moment 30 years ago

IV 14   Never try to talk sense to the senseless. Sense can't instruct them: but it can and it will infuriate them.

IV 16   Huxley's (*Island p. 260*) contrasted attitudes of mind — those who think in terms of either-or, and those who think of terms of not-only-but-also.

IV 18   *Huxley Island* p. 264 'his frantic and abhorred desires'. This note occurs so often in H's work that the dichotomy of feeling must have been verified many times in his own experience — and presumably is common or ordinary to people of certain temperaments. It baffles me (meaning a person of my, I suppose, different temperament). Reviewing *my* experience as carefully as I can, I don't recall ever having any such feeling. I've certainly 'desired', that is, liked or wanted, plenty of things which offended reason, justice, or decency, and acted accordingly. Impartially viewed, these acts might be 'abhorrent'; but not to *me*, or I simply wouldn't have wanted to do them. To do what I genuinely abhorred would be no more possible than not doing (if I saw the doing was practicable) what I 'desired' to do. In short, if I abhorred something I wouldn't want it; if I wanted it, I couldn't abhor it.

IV 21   S. hadn't seen the By Love Possessed film and when it turned up (second time around) at the Spring St. theatre today insisted on going. Seeing it a second time, I was again impressed by much really beautiful photography, and a number of excellences of small detail and minor casting — the man, whoever he was, cast as 'Dr. Shaw' in the trifling part allowed him was almost disconcerting, he was so exactly in face and manner what I was seeing as I wrote.* But it was as plain as ever that the job they undertook was impossible: the book defeated them at every turn and was indeed specifically intended to. A play, an acted entertainment by definition can't be 'honest' exhibiting True Experience. Actors act 'parts': plays must provide 'parts'. The whole basis is: Let's Pretend. Anything 'real' or 'true' will destroy or at any rate vitiate this basis. Life is life, not a play: a play is a play, not life. It seems to follow that an effective play must cut loose from considerations of: is this probable? (or even: is this possible?) and proceed on the principle of, say, *Hamlet*. Never mind whether this situation makes sense, never mind if it's obviously impossible. Assume it to be the situation: Now, what next?

*Everett Sloane. Ed.

IV 27 I'm amused to find myself still thinking back occasionally to that spew-out of Jewish fury that *By Love Possessed* provoked a few years ago — a kind of unfinished business in understanding, I can see. I don't like to leave such curiosities of human behavior not-thought-through. It's hard to see how anything actually stated in the text could provoke even annoyance, let alone a hardly-sane rage of abuse. Was there, then, something I could be read as implying? Did the real offense consist in the fact that the two Jewish lawyers mentioned were more or less peripheral (one never actually appearing at all); and the over-sensitive, suspicious, and silly, contrived to read into this a contempt or disdain, the more galling because it was unspoken, which simply dismissed Jews as beyond some pale, never considered admitting them to equality in the company of the chief characters? Once you began thinking this way, you might very well find yourself detecting injury and insult in the most innocent turn of phrase or casual reference. At any rate, that seems to be the best I can do for the moment.

V 1 A great many human activities don't interest me at all but why they interest others always does interest me.

V 16 For a man to be married more than twice, when it's a matter of divorce, is undignified and unbecoming, all possible explanations notwithstanding. He is declaring (a) he attaches too much importance to females (b) perhaps for that very reason, he can't get the use of one on the easier terms available to most men.

V 20 It seems in general true that a fool *can* always find a bigger fool to admire him.

V 27 Conrad Aiken and his wife who had been attending the Academy-Institute Annual Ceremonial in New York stopped by for dinner and the night. A little tight, perhaps (they travel with thermos bottles full of Martinis. I remember from their visit at Windingdale) but he was quite coherent enough about the whats, whys, and hows behind the grants, medals, and awards. He is on the joint Committee most concerned in the gold medal and perhaps truthfuly told how he got the fiction medal given to William Faulkner when Katherine Anne Porter had been going to get it; and the biography medal away from Matthew Josephson. I see no reason to doubt it's all strictly 'political' — you hand out to your friends and bilk your enemies; and I was able to see that one of the few smart things I've ever done was to keep out of it entirely, to have nothing to do with any of them. This is perhaps a little lofty; since, knowing Conrad was on the grants committee, I meant to fix matters for William Jay Smith. Breaking my rule, I recommended him to Mr. Coates, the chairman, when he wrote asking for suggestions, Prof. Allen having told me Smith could use it; and, also, irked by the run of odd-balls getting all the grants. I was served right, and my instruction confirmed. I had no sooner mentioned Smith's name (in the privacy of my study) when Conrad said: He's a shit. It developed that 8, yes 8, years ago Smith, in some poetry mag, had made little of Conrad Aiken, called him an unimportant poet. That comment, regardless of whether Smith's work had or hadn't merit, was going to cost him, or at least lose him, $2000. I took the liberty of saying I knew nothing about that; and hardly knew Smith; but I felt strongly that, on occasion, someone not odd-ball should be recognized; and personal considerations given less weight. I just barely managed, the word having been given me, *not* to say: 'Speaking of shits. . . .' of course this is not fair to Conrad — feeling the pain & rage he clearly felt is hard for me to understand; but if I had somehow been made to feel it, I have no right to think I'd be any more forgiving.

V 29   Anyone who enjoys any considerable success in this life must, unless he is a great fool (and of course, that is this point: he *can* be) recognize that merit never determines, nor even as far as you can honestly see, contributes to anything but small successes. There, it seems often essential. To make a thousand dollars you usually have to be fairly smart; to make a million, you must (a much rarer thing) be naturally lucky.

VI 5   You shall know the truth always by its banality. If it is new, it isn't true: if it is true, it isn't new.

some sad recollection of CA's conversation (supra V 27):
Item: Speaking of lingering winter in these hills, he mentioned that he had been at Concord, N. H. a few weeks ago and noticed snow remaining in all shaded places. This enabled him

to let it be known the S. Paul's School dramatic society had being putting on a play of his. [alas. how hungry for some notice a man must be if he troubles to go to see a secondary school play production and then troubles to let people know he did.

Item He related how he had gone and spoken to William Faulkner at the Institute 'Ceremonial' and Faulkner had respectfully quoted him some of his, C.', verses, only wrong. C. corrected him. F. firmly repeated them as he had first proposed them. Clearly, C said, a man of considerable determination [It was hard to doubt the incident was invented; and that the only point was to have it understood that Nobel Prize Winners got C's poetry by heart

VI 7   In the *New Yorker* Edmund Wilson has a piece which is a mock interview of himself by English journalists ('What is your opinion of So & So, Mr Wilson' etc). That this could strike him as a good or amusing idea perhaps says all. He speaks of "Somerset Maugham, a bad writer" Now the fact is, few writers have ever written English better. Wilson, who can often write well, can hardly help seeing this. Some expressed opinions of M's have, then, offended him. Offended, he loses all judgment. Among young writers, he considers good J.D. Salinger, Edwin O'Connor, and James Baldwin. In fact, compared to Maugham, all three in their different ways, write quite badly. Query: Why these plugs? What's in them, in point of psychopathic satisfaction, for Wilson?

VI 9   To understand her constant worrying about money when in fact she had all she needed you would have to realize the worry was a sort of sop to nemesis. To let her mind be easy, to admit to herself that she wasn't poor, would be bad luck, might be punished. So, piously, propitiatingly, she made herself worry. It was often hard to do, but fate must not be tempted. With determination she did it.

VI 12   (1 COR. 13:13) Now abideth faith, hope and money, these three: but the greatest of these is money.

VI 16   Charles Smith told me that he had been away because his mother had to be declared incompetent, she refusing to die despite strokes, heart attacks, and pathological conditions too numerous to mention. I found myself making my automatic response: Jolly, this life! etc. Thinking about it later, it occurred to me (for some reason, for the first time) that such sardonic or bitter cracks of mine are factitious in the sense that they base themselves on what I've seen happening to other people, not what has happened to me. So far, at least (a very considerable reservation, of course) I'd be hard put to find anything in my personal experience to justify my fault-finding, or to explain why I seem to feel that, given a choice in the matter, and knowing what I know now, no reasonable being would ever choose to be born.

VI 27   S. showed me a copy of July *Esquire* with a piece on Mary McCarthy by someone called Brock Brower rehearsing her literary and I guess marital career with some details I hadn't known but see no reason to doubt. You can't help wondering if it wasn't rather a pity that, right out of college, she was taken over, fell in with, the literary queers, the critical odd-balls, the pretentious pseudo-intellectuals and cockeyed communists; the Edmund Wilsons, the Philip Rhavs, the Dwight Macdonalds, who were posing and play-acting, and declining to grow up (of Wilson, she is quoted as saying: 'I believe he did cure me of liking Aldous Huxley'). It is true she survived them very well: but a little of their pretentiousness and literary smart-aleckry came off on her; and the truth isn't her quoted Chaucer line: 'I am myn owene woman, well at ese.'; she's still partly the *Partisan Review's* woman, and to that degree ill at ease indeed, and the worse for it.

VI 27   [the dreadfulness of *Esquire* in its new 'intellectualism' defies brief description. Norman Mailer on Mrs. Kennedy must be read to be believed — and even then you hardly believe in *him*: so prodigious an ass is surely not in nature. Then, there is the horror of Mrs. Parker's smart aleckry of senescence. On Porter's *Ship of Fools* (supra IV 12) "I never said it was a cheery book. I never said it was like those books that have so often been written about ship's companies — those bubbly bits of gaiety on the high seas [name one] But I do say, and I think I shall go on saying: My God, here is a book!" [I'll just bet she'll go on saying that: and, God help her, saying it that way.

VII 6   In view of VII 1 supra*, William Faulkner's sudden taking-off gave me the least little bit of a turn of the nihil nisi bonum kind; and the newspaper consensus does seem to indicate that I'm about the only person in the world who wasn't edified by his later-day high-falutin sentiments. HT. headline: *'Spoke to Heart of all – Kennedy on Faulkner'* The President: "It can be said with assurance of few men in any area of human activity [this could be F. himself writing] that their work will long endure. William Faulkner was one of these men. Since Henry James no author has left such a vast and enduring monument to the strength of American literature, etc"
[If I feel strong doubt about the 'enduring' of the monument it is, of course, because I lost patience with *Sanctuary* thirty years ago; and after (I think) *'The Wild Palms'* stopped even trying to

---

*Cozzens had quoted from Faulkner's Nobel Prize address, noting "no comment seems possible".

read him. What had been to me the wonderful, the highly exciting, vigor and effectiveness of the work he was doing in the first books seemed to end with *As I Lay Dying*. This could of course mean a change in my own tastes or interests; but I don't think so. *Sanctuary* shocked me by the cheapness of thinking and feeling — the last thing I had expected. In the next books I found him developing further and further a style, very tiresome to read, whose office appeared to be concealing under piles of words the shoddiness or childishness of what he had to say. It is perfectly true that many, perhaps most, of the realities of this life's complicated thinking and feeling can't be got at with simple statements. To simplify will be to falsify And I'm also sure F. was honestly wrestling with Marlowe's 'One thought, one grace, one wonder at the least / Which into words no virtue can digest' — the hope most writers surely have to make words say more than words are able to say. The result of this effort is usually (Joyce is the perfect example) and, indeed, you have to see, inevitably, that you will convey less meaning, not more, when you tamper with the language, whether the words themselves, or the structure of the sentences. So I don't agree with the President (and the rest of the world). What will 'endure' seems likely to be what *has* endured. Should Jane Austen perhaps be an object lesson for the kind of writer able to thirst after 'immortality'? (I can't myself seem to give a damn about posterity's opinion).

VII 10 Ken McCormick sent S. a copy of Herman Wouk's *Youngblood Hawke* which I've been reading (finally) with a kind of distress. The author is earnest and honest, and a hell of a hard worker at piling up 783 pages. From the tripe, which may be to say, practical standpoint there very well may be a good subject for book club boobs in the 'romance' of someone like the late Thomas Wolfe — big books, big play-acting, big money, hell-raising and a lot of dames rolling right over. What the truth of all this may have been like for Wolfe one easily guesses was probably pretty grim. Wouk might be said to half-see, in a blurred way, suspect, sometimes even hint at, something not on the boob level: but as he writes along you see, alas that earnest or not, honest or not, the boob level is his own level: and, alas, again, as Aldous Huxley once pointed out, hard work can never be a substitute for real talent.

VII 12 *TLS 29/VI/62* Middle. *Time's Laughing Stocks* "... This device, through which action is carried on through casual asides [Waugh: *Decline & Fall* Lord Tangent] is derived directly from Firbank ... It would be difficult to say just when Mr. Waugh decided that this technique was inadequate for the things he wanted to say ... Firbankian comedy is serious in its own way, but ... tracing 'the workings of the divine purpose in

a pagan world' which has been Mr. Waugh's principal concern
since 1945 is one [of the things it cannot do]: "[But, oh my
God, you think: Why did he have to turn to this crap about
'workings of divine providence'? That is perhaps the real point
and the real explanation. His peculiar powers of imagination
couldn't be confined to his writing. He lived with them; and
since he was a homosexual, he was presently going Catholic,
going where private or individual imaginings were more or less
lost or resolved in a grand general scheme of imaginings, that it
ruined him as a writer seems indiputable: but what the hell.
True, as he is quoted (in 1929): 'the novel should be directed
for entertainment'; but the novelist also has himself to think
about. Let readers take their chance: or, in brief: *Screw You
Jack*: in Catholicism (or whatever other nonsense he finds
emotionally satisfying) *I've Got Mine*. Still, as a reader one can
wish he hadn't had to do it.

VII 15   having as a writer, been myself in that somewhat uncomfortable yet essentially comic-opera situation: *He's the guy they all
abuse / Both the Catholics and the Jews*

The ordinary high-tone pronouncement that Sex isn't Everything is very true; but those who make it may be guessed, as a
rule, to mean: Sex isn't (they wish, they wish) Anything. Henry
Miller's not very interesting books seem to provoke the pronouncement often: so let us grant that a man must eat before he
can fuck; and he must have money before he can eat, and he
must work before he can have money; but in the case of the
average man it would be absurd to think working, making
money, and eating can absorb him in anything like the way
fucking can absorb him.

VII 17   *TIME* on the French 'neo-realists': "They do not bother to
describe sex in morbid detail. That alone, if it catches on, could
set the novel ahead ten years." See (and how quickly, supra VII
15 (2). The 'catching on' is of course the point. After Henry
Miller, already pretty much deja vue when the censors let him
go on sale, why No Sex may be going to be the thing of the
moment: but except in terms of the vogue, it will surely leave
the novel just where it found it (and Sex just where it always is).

VII 18   S. brought me a ball pen of hers which she said wouldn't work.
It seemed to work for me all right so, to prove it, I wrote on my
scratch pad: *Bernice is a bad girl*. Giggling she grabbed the pen
and wrote firmly under it: *No, she isn't!* Through and under the
bit of kidding I could see, it seemed to me, in that instant,
automatic, quick-as-thought written rejoinder an expression
quite unrelated to kidding, of that wonderful sense of righteousness, of self-justification which no woman fails to have.
Driven into a corner, men, or some men, even most men, give

way, admit they were wrong, mistaken, or ought to have done differently, because they have see that so they were or so they should. Has any female ever, under any circumstances, conceded about herself or any act of hers anything of the kind? This isn't hypocrisy: she just can't *see* herself as 'a bad girl', no matter what she does.

5   24 July 1962-22 January 1963

VII 25   Either he knows his statement to be false, and so, is a liar; or he believes it true, and so, is a fool.

VII 26   You may rightly expect women of real learning to be more or less manish. An attractive femininity must seem unplanned and effortless: but this will be art concealing art. The cultivation and care of female charm is in fact the next thing to a full-time job. If she is to be and to remain charming how can a woman fit into her days (and nights) those innumerable hours of concentrated study on which real learning has to rest? For most women, the answer will be: she can't. If she's scholarly, she isn't going to be charming. If she's charming, she isn't going to be scholarly. It's a mere matter of 60 minutes making an hour and 24 hours making a day.

VII 27   The observable fact that among the nice things loved by men who love nice things are pretty boys more often than pretty girls.

VII 29   *Why Writers should shut up.* John O'Hara again in LN's NYT column: 'I haven't had a drink in nine years.' Could that be what's making his later books more and more labored and less and less worth reading? One thinks of Upton Sinclair, the great teetotaler, and his flux of simply God-awful 'novels'.

Aldous Huxley's suggestion (by Francis Chelifer in *Those Barren Leaves*) that: This game of art resembles conjuring. The quickness of the tongue deceives the brain

VIII 4   The truth about him seems to be that truth about Charles Sumner said to have been proposed by a Boston lady. Sumner, she said, was 'a specimen of prolonged and morbid juvenility'.

VIII 5   It is written that the love of money is the root of all evil. The assertion's absurdity to any reflective reader surely suggests a slip of the pen. For 'love' read 'lack,' and the passage immediately makes sense, states a truth, sets out an important fact of life.

VIII 7   If the offence is evidentially established in law one need not establish a motive: yet in life men are seldom content with mere findings of fact. To the question: What was the big idea? they want some answer. Perhaps this is a matter of subconscious anxiety and alarm stirring when any act is unexplained. To allow that things may happen, or be done, for *no* reason — this way madness lies.

VIII 10 Nicholson *Tennyson* pp 265-271. N. considers T.'s religious views with considerable penetration and good illustration. You seem to see 'Faith' boiled down to what it always has to be — the childish wish-hope, the unadult persuasion, that the observed disagreeable fact — all men have died and you'll be next — can be exorcised or excepted to by professing certain beliefs in stories that are improbable and claims that are impossible, by performing certain venerable rituals, by adhering (in what degree you can) to prescribed patterns of conduct. Your physical death, though not made a bit less certain, may this way (you manage to tell yourself) be kept from being what death looks so much like — the absolute end of the man dying — "the black negation of the bier."

[As a great believer through experience in the proposition: Malt does more that Milton can / To justify God's ways to man, a horrible pun here oppresses me. How about: The bright negation of the beer? Put down a couple pints: and who's afraid of big, bad death?

[p. 271 quote from T. "I would rather know that I was to be lost eternally than not to know that the human race was to live eternally." A kind of pathos of self-justification: even if it includes me out: please let the possibility be true. I 'would rather' take my chances than think there were no chances at all; so I'm going to believe no matter what.

ibid. p. 217 "The last years of his life were clouded by ill health and domestic bereavements." [most unusual?]

VIII 11 *Letters of James Agee to Father Flye* A Robert Phelps in a preface: "Certainly thus much seems to me true: nothing that Agee wrote . . . expresses his temperament any better or more memorably than . . . such letters as those to be found in the present book." Affirmed, alas, as stated. One guesses that Agee had qualities of personal charm, if of a rather off-beat or sentimental kind, so that those who knew him can read extra meaning into what those who didn't know him would be apt to find quite ordinary and often tiresome. Of course I have to recognize that I'm alienated a good deal by his persisting ability to treat seriously, though a grown man — or, no: that's it perhaps. He never really got to be that — little Anglo-Catholic problems of faith or order. On 25 October 1932 he asks that he and the Olivia he is marrying be remembered at Father F.'s mass the morning of their wedding day. It is certainly bias to see childishness in this serious request; but see it I'm afraid I do.

p. 84. "Things have to be believed with the body, or in other words, soul: not just perceived of the mind." This seems a good statement of his everyday attitude of temperament. But if you aren't of the same temperament, you want to say: no, no, no! Stand by what's 'perceived of the mind'. The body's 'belief' is just an emotional mood of the moment and you shouldn't indulge it.

p. 109 "The human race is incurably sick." [When you find yourself believing that, guess who's really sick.

VIII 12   The Death of Santa Claus. Weidman *The Sound of Bow Bells* p. 248 et seq "the disappointment of fulfillment". But to experience this, you have to be childish all your life, a real simpleton, don't you?

VIII 15   A little watching of and listening to the prudish will convince you that their 'good taste' in avoiding 'unpleasant subjects' manifests not 'refinement' but pure and simple inappetency. Head shaking at pleasure's name is quite certain to mean that the head-shakers are themselves physiologically or psychologically prevented from experiencing such pleasure.

VIII 17   *FORM LETTER* I've long felt that any novelist's estimate of a novel is bound to be so limited and conditioned by the kind of work he finds himself able to do that opinions he may form about another novelist's novel are worthless: and he should always keep them to himself.

VIII 21   *NY Times Book Review L.N.'s page* [more on supra VII 29] Mr James T. Farrell is reported as living a life in which "an occasional debauch consists of a coke at a neighborhood bar". Mr. Farrell on the point: "A good many American writers drink themselves to death. I am going out sober." [a writer who hadn't done a lot of drinking in his time would hardly be likely to come up with this kind of resolution. Presumably the drinking was done back when he was doing his writing. Since he was always a dreadful writer, the proposition, so strongly suggested by Upton Sinclair's case, that good writing depends in some way on drinking, seems shaken. Who knows? Perhaps you need talent too.

VIII 22   Speaking of the things to be said for age, I've thought of another; and, I fear, poor one. You do get to be able to read through a newspaper and judge with rarely an error what could just possibly be true in news stories; and what is got wrong, what is made up, and what is patent nonsense, like a prepared handout which is covering up the truth, not telling it.

VIII 26   Another note on *The Sound of Bow Bells* (p. 343) That romanticism of self-pity may perhaps be seen in these passages that argue (I would think rightly that a writer seldom knows how he did whatever he does. But the implication that 'success' has to be a matter of 'merit' is absurd. All you have to do to see this is to note what *has* paid off for other writers. Clearly, the process is hardly different from feeding coins into a slot machine. Of course, the coins probably have to be real and current coins: but the one that releases the jackpot doesn't do it because it is 'better' than previously inserted coins. The book that pays off may be good: but it doesn't *have* to be; and since bad or indifferent books will always greatly outnumber good books; more often than not the jackpot is hit by a book without much merit.

IX 1   His stories made you think of the ludicrous, so often pathetically unbelieveable, lies that a child, too limited in experience that teaches you how to invent stories which really might be true, will often try to tell.

IX 6   Shirley Jackson. *We Have Always Lived in the Castle* The writing technique of the calculated hold-out on the reader is nothing but ill-advised. That the effectiveness of having the reader 'suddenly come to realize' may momentarily be great doesn't change the fact that the effect is momentary. The serious reader must see that you have cheated; and you have gravely damaged what might be called your credit, the indispensible factor in persuading him to suspend his disbelief. Tempting as such devices may seem, they're self-defeating. Like it or not, you can't do better than start at the beginning, not at the middle, or the end; come clean; lay your cards on the table. "I was born in the year 1632, in the city of York, of a good family etc"* [I wish I could remember this.

*From *Robinson Crusoe.* See *Morning Noon and Night,* p. 402. Ed.

IX 8   *Critical Comedy* Perhaps in reaction to the panning they gave his second book (itself, no doubt, reaction to the ridiculous praise they gave his first) some critics seem to have decided they will find merit in James Jones' new novel if it kills them. And it almost does. The obvious stubborn fact that they undertake to gloss shows between most of their lines. What they're resolved to speak well of is, clearly, thinking as infantile and writing as abysmally bad as ever. Gannet *H.T.* "Such understanding is the beginning of wisdom, without which no book, however 'readable' becomes literature" Geismar *Times* "He has apparently remained impervious to all temptations of popular and commercial success; he had kept his integrity, his own vision of life. And he proves his talent and his integrity once again with *The Thin Red Line.*" [i. e: Mr. J. makes here no effort to be anything but the very bad writer he naturally is.

Curiosities of Coincidence (or Something). Baby-sitting at F's* Pownal shop while the girls attended an auction, I entertained five visitors (one buying $3 worth). The fifth arrival was a Chrysler with Pa. plate. The couple who came in said they were dealers looking for clocks; but only French gilt ones. Perhaps because I had come downstairs with a book in my hand to keep my place, the woman, taking me to be a reader, said: What we want is — well, there was novel a few years ago, did you happen to see it, called By Love Possessed; and it had a jacket with the picture of the kind of clock I mean. I said: Yes, I saw it. I knew what she meant. But I was afraid Mrs. Collins didn't have any of those.

*Fannie Collins, Bernice Cozzens's sister, operated an antique shop in Vermont near Williamstown.

IX 29

One T.R. Martland, an assistant professor of religion (what a wonderful title) at Lafayette College, has a *Living Church* piece on: *Hemingway – If he was Fair to Religion, is Christianity true to Christ?* The line of the argument seems to be: "As H. sees it, religion's role is to make life easier . . . Religion and God exist to serve man . . . In his passionate concern to observe life and record it faithfully was H. fair to the phenomena of religion? Perhaps a more serious question: if H. is a faithful recorder, is Christianity being true to Christ?" [in the 'more serious question' the assistant prof.'s meaning isn't altogether clear to me. Does he wish to say Christ never proposed or promised to be 'useful'? That would seem to be true; though surely, if you have a soul to save, saving it could be called 'useful'. Does he wish to say that 'Christianity' as now constituted fails in usefulness because Christ's precepts are at least somewhat neglected? A phrasing of the prof's, 'the inept god of organized religion' might suggest he meant the latter. But, speaking of More Serious Questions, the effect got here by assembling a collection (11) of quotes is in some ways appalling. They seem to serve to bring out a persistent and consistent non-adult attitude, a cheapness of feeling, that was slurred over to some degree when they came in context and H's real narrative and descriptive gifts could sometimes carry you past them with no more than pricks of uneasiness or embarrassment. That this kind of thing (though of course its badness is aggravated when passages pages and years apart are crammed together: Yet alas you are made this way to see that there was no growing-up in all that time, nothing learned, nothing forgotten] could have been seriously regarded as the 'essence of reality) by most of a whole literary generation must be a sobering consideration. [IN R FILE]

X 2

In *Panorama*, a magazine of Bucks County Les. Trauch sent me for its new court house story, random fillers at column bottoms included two quotes from Mark Twain:

"There are several good protections against temptation; but the surest is cowardice."

"It takes your enemy and your friend working together to hurt you to the heart: the one to slander you, the other to get the news to you."

[This hurt-to-the-heart business (supra: Priestly) suggests to me that as writers go I'm indeed singularly unfeeling. The late-in-the day abuse given *By Love Possessed* was surely about as stupid and venomous as abuse can get; and it's true [supra IX 25]* I was taken aback, and even perhaps fatuously 'aggrieved' because most of it seemed to me 'unfair'. But 'hurt' I certainly wasn't. I don't know whether this was because all the 'abuse' I saw was unmistakably partisan, by an angry Jew or an angry Catholic (and, 'at heart' I'm afraid my feeling is: who cares a hoot about that kind of basically dishonest crap?); or whether I'm just so damn (and beyond reason) conceited that I can feel: if they don't like me, so much the worse for them. Whatever it is: the only time I can remember needing to lick wounds was when the N. Y. Times reviewer said quite rightly in 1924 that my first book was no good. [but Clemens wasn't wrong. It was I remember, shown me by my then 'friend' Lucius Beebe with a pleasure impossible for him to conceal.]

*Cozzens's reaction to a comment by Norman Podhoretz in *Show* that Cozzens's "reputation was utterly destroyed by Dwight Macdonald's famous article in *Commentary*."

X 6   In connection with X 2 supra one other point or perhaps factor occurred to me. Everyone who 'abused' me also had something to say about what he thought was good in writing. When you find that what they admire is the kind of crap Norman Mailer writes (for instance) you can't have too much trouble feeling their critical opinion doesn't matter. If they thought or spoke well of anyone who was any good, I suppose this might not be so easy. [but, looking back, I see I did make this point. Could I be, as well as senile, getting sensitive? I don't think so. I must have read something, I forget what, that suggested the point — or, is that senility?

X 15   Checking a point I thought I remembered in Elizabeth Bowen's *Death of the Heart* I came on one of what desultory re-reading shows me were far too many passages like this (p. 385): "Happy that few of us are aware of the world until we are already in league with it. Childish fantasy, like the sheath over the bud not only protects but curbs the terrible budding spirit, protects not only innocence from the world but the world from the power of innocence." [a.) what is: in league with the world? b) how do you 'curb' a budding spirit; and what is terrible about that spirit? c) what is the 'power of innocence'? — Just, you might say, answer yes or no.

X 17   In *Forbes* on an often painful last page called *Thoughts on the Business of Life* (edifying quotes) is one from the late William Faulkner which somewhat rocked me back. The long line of his tiresome later books had made me stop reading him as much as twenty years ago because it seemed unlikely he would write anything more worth my reading. But: "when grown people speak of the innocence of children, they don't really know what they mean. Pressed, they will go a step further and say; well, ignorance, then. The child is neither. There is no crime that a boy of 11 has not envisaged long ago. His only innocence is he may not yet be old enough to desire the fruits of it. His ignorance is, he does not know how to commit it" (source of quote not given)
[The faults of F.'s writing, the imprecision that makes you tired, comes out, to be sure, when he puts down 'the child is neither' never bothering to notice 'has neither' is needed. Of course he doesn't mean 'envisaged' because he goes right on to say there's been no confrontation. The 'long ago' is simply unconsidered. The 'boy of 11' makes it silly. No doubt that boy has already thought about the 'crimes'; but at his age it wouldn't be 'long ago' at all. Still, there is a distillation of truth, even if obvious truth, of the kind that makes writing worth reading and I'd forgotten — it was what made his first books so exciting — that F. had it in him.

X 28   In the *NY Times Mag* a piece by Thomas Hart Benton which of course defended his own work if only decently and indirectly and merely said [speaking of a Braque, or Kandinsky 'pattern'] "However there is something unreal, high falutin and a little naive woven through most of this crusading . . ."
[I don't know how the element of the obvious phony could be put better: and the ill ease with words — words being not a painter's job — somehow make it more effective in stating a truth that seems to go to all arts; not least, writing. The thought seems to tie in with Mr. Steinbeck's Nobel Prize. How appropriate in it's way: yet must crap and clap-trap; the 'unreal, high falutin and the naive' be given prizes? Ans: yes; and rightly. Prizes are bad in that they are always given not for merit, but against somebody. The only reason I got a Pulitzer prize was not because I 'deserved' it (though that year I certainly did) but because that year the 'judges' were mad at other more likely candidates; and not for the reason that their books were bad (which they were) but because I happened to offend them less. (I would have been glad to offend them more, if only I'd known I was in danger of 'winning'.)

XI 3   Strunk & White *Elements of Style*. On back of paperback:

Strunk: 'This book aims to give in brief space the principal requirements of plain English style.' E.B. White 'I shall [Strunk taught him that] have a word or two to say about attitudes in writing: the how, the why, the bear traps, the power, and the glory.'] [He taught himself that] Dorothy Parker: 'It is a book to put alongside Fowler's works: and I can think of no higher praise'. [Could she ever have read 'Fowler's works'?]
[on all obvious points the 'aim' certainly seems well directed. Simplicity (don't say: *He is a man who is very ambitious*. Say: *He is very ambitious*) and clarity get proper emphasis: but both author and editor seem often to let their enthusiasm for 'simplicity' lead them to suppose it the same as clarity. The simple can't help being clear: but that doesn't mean it won't be also nonsense, or untruth. The simple manner is always good: but matter, not manner, is the important thing. If 'simplicity' involves any sacrifice of the truth, of the significance, of a statement, simplicity just isn't worth it. When, for instance, you insist that something is either 'likely' or 'unlikely' you make for inexactness. 'Unlikely' isn't quite the same as 'not likely'; 'likely' is not quite the same as 'not unlikely'. Advice to avoid such distinctions of meaning in writing is bad advice.

XI 8   A lawyer from Picayune (I'll say nothing about that) Missis-sippi writes me to say he feels that I, not Mr. Steinbeck ought to have had the Nobel prize, and avoids undue solemnity by adding: 'I intend to see you are suitably rewarded in 1963 if I have to establish the (Emil J.) Gex (Jr) prize.' I was at least led to review again my feeling that there's nothing I'd like less than the Nobel Prize: and no, there isn't anything I'd like less. By published accounts, Mr. S. got no warning (I suppose a fac-tional fight went on among, you assume, non-English-reading Swedes) and was simply notified one morning he'd been chosen the night before. Getting any such cable, what a hell of a spot I would have found myself on. Can you refuse? Think of the news story *that*'s going to make. Can you accept something that has been worse than meaningless, really affrontive, ever since the award went to Pearl Buck? I relieved my imagined state of mind a little by composing an answering cable: *Glad to have money if you want to forward it. Can't see my way to going to Stockholm for less than $100,000. Are you interested?* Even in imagination, I could be sure that S., fortunately, would never let me send it.

XI 11   Anthony Powell. *The Kindly Ones*. It's obvious that a writer saves himself a lot of work if he writes successive books about the same characters: but this latest Powell suggests to me that for reasons of a more or less mysterious kind, going perhaps to the springs, sources, or basic mechanics of 'creative writing' a writer's well-advised not to do it. First: the books tend to become parts of a serial. Each stands less and less on its own feet: and I very much doubt that when the series is done and they're taken all together they'll cohere into any kind of whole. Second: I suspect the writer may need the renewed exercise of having each time to create from scratch a new world, or at any rate, new people. To use the same old ones is perhaps to let his imagination get flabby: and this will mar the quality or tone of the writing itself in some no doubt subtle way. In the present book, you seem to see both factors working. The narrative backs firmness and coherence. The material, though still here and there good, is too often listless sounding; or, bluntly, dull.

XI 13   Everyone I know seems to be dying: and I don't even know many people

XI 17   To take romance out of things, there's nothing like good eyesight

XI 18   *Connel: Palmerston p. 153* quoting Dr. Johnson: On a line from an ode of Whitehead's 'Who rules o'er Free men should himself be free.' " 'No, sir,' says Johnson 'there's nothing in this. Billy Whitehead, to be sure, is a pretty tinkling poet: but the line you have mentioned has no merit. The thought is false: and I might as well say: 'who drives fat oxen should himself be fat.' "
[I wonder if anyone who ever enjoyed a really great literary reputation in his own time had stood up as well as Johnson. Nearly two hundred years later, with all kinds of fads and fashions passing, he can still arrest you with a justness of phrasing and of adult perception that makes you see his credit wasn't a bit more than his desert.
[on the point of 'reputation' and what besides Dr. Johnson's abilities may create it, one may think of that of Robert Frost today, since his verse is mostly much like 'Billy Whitehead's' as Johnson saw that. That factor of longevity clearly works, just as Maugham suggested in *Cakes & Ale*. In popular acceptance, living on becomes genius. (Cf. Walt Whitman's metamorphosis from a writer virtually unread (and of course continuing to be unread) into the Good Grey Poet)

XI 19   Is it odd, or is it only natural, that a man who has the courage to kill himself when he is persuaded his life is no longer worth living is called cowardly; while a man who elects to let himself be kept alive, a burden to himself and everyone else (and for what believable reason but that he's afraid to die?) is called courageous?

XII 1   He said: "There's no excuse for that—unless, of course I did it myself"

XII 3   Unfortunately for friends of reason, a lesson of experience is that absurdity doesn't have to mean untruth. What is too absurd to credit can turn out to be the fact of the matter, almost any matter; and the longer you've lived, the oftener you'll have found this to be the sad case.

XII 4 Running into him on Spring Street as I went into Bemis' to get the papers, I had a Bob & Jim exchange with Professor Allen, Chairman of the English Department (and a very agreeable man; and I'm quite sure a very good one at his job; any snide sound above was inadvertant and unintended: my god, how language always needs watching) and he wanted to know if I'd have time to do some second semester 'consulting' with undergraduates in the Creative Writing courses, as last year—the 'second semester' point being a matter of 'screening', he and Bill Smith having decided by then who, if anyone, had what seemed to them 'promise'. I said yes: I'd see by appointment at Mather House on one or more afternoons a week anyone who wanted to see me. I managed not to say: only, is it worth their time? I have nothing to tell them except that writing is a long, hard, often dirty, and in most cases, unremunerative business; and all you'll ever learn is what you can teach yourself etc. etc. It occurred to me afterward that, while every bit of that is true, and so certainly didn't need saying, there might possibly be one approach in which 'teaching' could be of value (Not that I'd want to try it). A course that confinded itself to a study, not of excellence in writing, but of the ways of going wrong, conceivably could save a would-be writer some time. You could point out to him, by simply exhibiting examples, a few of the things that his inexperience might make him attempt, in that hope of extra or larger or more exact communication which no one who writes seriously can help having; but which aren't going to work. At random, out of order, and with none of the careful consideration a proper list would need, some examples to exhibit might include: (of course I don't suggest any of these should be read all the way through: a few pages of each ought to be enough) Carlyle's *French Revolution* (Keep Calm): Pater's *Marius the Epicurean* (but don't be phoney about it); Twain's *Huckleberry Finn* (watch your 'comedy': that king and duke stuff, for example, you don't want): Joyce's *Ulysses* (don't fool with the English language; you can't win; Pearl Buck *The Good Earth* (never try to be biblical); Steinbeck: *Cannery Row* (don't be maudlin); Hemingway's *Across the River and into the Trees* (check yourself for childishness); Shirley Jackson *The Haunting of Hill House* (trying to say things by not saying them is not a good idea); Dreiser's *An American Tragedy* (You can't get away with never learning to write); Norman Mailer *The Naked and the Dead*. (Feeling is no substitute for fact); Virginia Woolf *Orlando* (let symbolism alone). I'm sure better examples could be found in a number of cases: but I think each of these can be said to have a learnable lesson about writing and a young writer who was taught them effectively would really be ahead in the game that interests him.

XII 23   The mistaken notion that what is simple must somehow be synonymous with what is good, that simplicity purifies itself, as running water was once supposed to. In fact, the essence of the simple is generally imperception; and what it shows most of the time, at least in practice, is sometimes sheer incapacity and sometimes shiftless laziness. It's not at all a rejection of the pretentious or the affected. Pretentiousness and affectation, however futile and tiresome, are hard work. They involve reflection, an exercise of judgment, and the capacity to take pains. The man of good sense sees that the possible fruits of this labor can't possibly justify the trouble he would have to go to; he'll tend to be as 'simple' as circumstances permit, because wasting time can't make good sense. But if he has some unfortunate need to practice to deceive, good sense will also tell him: be simple. Simplicity is the lie's best friend.

XII 24   He seemed to have none of that safeguarding knowledge of life and men so necessary if you are to go into matters outside your understanding and experience. You might think of him, ignorant of danger, as a mouse at the trap. What can a mouse know about man-made infernal machines? Unerring, he has come where a scent of that delicacy, the bait, drew him. With triumph, he regards his prize. With relish he starts nibbling: and—wham!

XII 31   *Not spoken in criticism.* The observable, wonderful sense of righteousness that seems innate—that is: wholly unfaked, quite unstudied—in almost every woman is perhaps the cardinal factor in making female behaviour so often baffling to men? That men *are* baffled seems proof positive that, whatever the sense actually consists in, men as a rule lack it: and so, also, that it's different from, ought not to be confused with, vanity, conceit, self-interest, or the habit of thinking unwarrantably well of oneself, which men by no means lack and couldn't find at all baffling [cf 4 VII 18]

I 7   Could it be possible that you'll always do better doing whatever you damn well please, than by doing what you yourself, or someone else, tries to tell you you ought to do?

I 9   The National Institute of Arts & Letters, sending out its final ballot for new candidates seems now to have returned without explanation to the yes and no form that was dropped as I remember, a number of years ago. One has to conclude that the opportunity to blackball personal enemies (cf. Conrad Aiken 4

V 7) was very dear to the rank and file. Just not voting *for* someone of whom they were jealous, or who had offended them by criticizing them unfavorably, didn't properly serve revenge's purpose. It should be possible to hurt the chances of such a 'shit', not merely leave them unhelped. My first thought on these occasions is: twenty years of this is enough. I resign. My second is: and if you do, you're really acting exactly like them. Is that what you want?

I 11 Suicide Note "I don't like it here: so I've gone back where I came from."

6   25 January 1963-19 August 1963

I 26 *ART IN AMERICA no 1 1963* presents a 50th Anniversary Number on the 1913 'Armory Show' with some interesting comment by survivors and 'background material'. If I had any competence in, or real feeling about, 'Art' I wouldn't, I remind myself, line my study with rows of Currier & Ives civil war prints: so that's the last word on that. But the various recounts, all aesthetics aside, have a perhaps horrid fascination in showing you the almost incredibly absurd seriousness with which the practitioners, both academic and 'rebel,' seem to have taken themselves. I'd always realized that the absurdity and conceit of writers, while certainly on many occasions repulsive, was almost modesty compared to what actors and musicians could show. But I hadn't realized, never I suppose being enough interested in 'Art' to pay attention to painters, that *they* can make singers and actors seem modest. I suppose the simple fact is: root hog, or die. Writers don't have to root quite as hard as people on the stage or in music; while *they* don't have to root in the desperate way every painter and sculptor has to.

I 29 Robert Frost seems finally to have been allowed to die this morning after Peter Bent Bingham spent a last-word-in-medical-science-month on the poor 88 year old bastard. President Kennedy is reported as pronouncing: 'There is a vacancy in the American Spirit' The interesting literary point is surely Somerset Maugham's 'longevity' point. Ten years ago, Frost got no attention of any serious critical kind—indeed his verse had often a little or a lot in common with that of the late Edgar Guest; and was mostly written off. But he kept living; and soon 'Publicity' got behind him—really, exactly like Walt Whitman (read, most of his life, by almost no one) living on until he got to be the Good Gray Poet; and had finally (and in spite of the Catholic hierarchy squawks, showing you how the inertia of a popular idea can meet and lick even its equal) the latest Camden-Philadelphia bridge named for, or after, him.

I 30   Just as no amount of work takes the place of talent, no amount of talent takes the place of work.

II 2   That modern architecture whose generally admired latest structures persist in looking to me like capsized boats, cocked hats, or at best, enormous filing cases.

II 8   *TLS 25 Jan.* Almost a page is given to the study (apparently in Swedish) by a Swede (one Alvar Ellegård) entitled: *Who was Junius? A Statistical Method of Determining Authorship.* What he seems to have set himself to do was feed a computer with figures on the frequency of certain phrases in the *Letters* and set it to work out from the frequency of such phrases in writings of people who could possibly have been 'Junius' who Junius must have been. The thing seems fantastic to a point of high farce. Today could anyone, let alone people whose language was Swedish, give a solitary good god damn who Junius was? But: "Mr. Ellegård carefully avoided another pitfall: many of the characteristics of Junian (sic) style might be common to political pamphleteers. . . After eliminating words that were decidedly plus or minus in these types of writing. . . [he] was left with 272 items in his testing list, representing only 1.8 percent of occurrences in the million-word general sample and 2.5 percent of the Junius material. . ." And the scientific finding? It ends where Macaulay with no computer began. It was probably Sir Philip Francis. I'd always thought 'James Joyce Scholarship' was as crazy as you could get. I must now wonder.

II 12   *Berkshire Eagle advt. Church of Christ*: quotes Edwin Conklin 'a noted biologist' in Jan. *Reader's Digest* "The probability of life originating from an accident is comparable to the probability of the unabridged dictionary resulting from an explosion in a print shop." [The undying popularity of the argument from design, the teleological 'proof', with the religiously inclined is probably worth more study than I have the wit, time, or inclination to give it. Surely it's a sign of something; tells you a lot about the religious temperament which is able to see it as somehow conclusive—either you deny the complexity of the universe (do you or don't you?); or, (since they're right: no rational person could deny it) you admit it. If you admit it, what can follow but whatever they happen to believe? But if you don't have the religious temperament, the wish or will to believe what they happen to believe, you find yourself more or less staggered by what seems to you the fallacy so evident that surely (you think) no one able to think at all could accept it. The analogy seems not merely false but simply preposterous. Why do you think it improbable that an explosion in a print shop would produce the unabridged dictionary? Because of course you deal with data you have or can easily get. A print shop amounts to an ascertainable fact: and so does an unabridged dictionary: and so in fact does an explosion—even if it must be granted that an explosion in a print shop isn't so every day an occurrence that you 'know' the results in that case. But what do you know of 'life' except that you yourself seem to be what's called 'alive'? About life's actual origins, you know absolutely nothing at all. How can there be the slightest correspondence in degrees of 'probability' between the one and the other? If this kind of 'proof' proves anything to the unbelieving tempera-ment, what can it be but that any eyewash will do if you need to believe what you need to believe? [of course I must repeat that as I get older and older and see more and more of the phenome-non of religion, I can't and don't mean anything pejorative in that kind of conclusion. Stupidity isn't here opposing sense; nor learning, ignorance: nor (perhaps) even thinking, feeling. That is; I've certainly seen that stupidity, ignorance, and 'feel-ing' are quite as compatible with Unbelief as with Belief. If experience suggests they're more often compatible with Belief, the finding's merely pragmatic. You may treat it as probably true; but you must not take it for a last absolute truth.

II 24   In the *New Yorker* Edmund Wilson makes a fairly disturbing use of a new book by Morley Callaghan about Paris in Those Days* to beat what you can't help concluding is soured and disappointed senility (I remember the silly, pompous business, some back, of his grave lapse in judgment in supposing a mock 'interview' of himself was a good idea) has now turned into beating dogs with any stick. He writes: "I remember—to give a few reminiscences of my own—seeing Hemingway etc etc, seeing Fitzgerald etc, etc . . ." The matter introduced seems to serve no purpose but to make himself into an amused aloof spectator, worth in intellect and literary ability the whole lot of them (only nobody then or now seems to realize it). He writes: "I never could understand how so many people got the idea from his books that Hemingway was a hard boiled charac-ter . . ." [Mercy me, you might say: did anyone of any judg-ment ever doubt that H's great writing talent was constantly being vitiated by a sentimentality next perhaps to John Stein-beck's, the sincerest and so in effect the phoniest of our time?

That Summer in Paris (New York: Coward-McCann, 1963). Ed.

III 5   One thing you seem to learn from all (well, at any rate, most) now 'reformed' Communists among our self-designated intel-lectuals is that their 'communism' was never anything much but an expression, you might even say a symptom, of a basic temperamental or emotional disorder. The disorder seems to have been in every case a curious non-adult capacity to accept unreal views of life which, for reasons whether of temperament, or perhaps more often, of traumatic personal experience of a social kind, appealed to them. They were satisfying emotional needs and no matters of principle or reasonable conviction were seriously involved. When communism stopped being a distinction of difference, in their own eyes very high-brow, and became a pretty risky profession they could leave it in a hurry and with no real trouble of mind. It had been their refuge from the facts of life. It couldn't go on being that with the party more or less outlawed as a foreign agent and with the police coming. Now, in communism, you didn't escape from, you were forced to face, facts of life. To stand your ground, to quit yourselves like men would be absurd, a negation of all communism. But of course the disorder was left uncured. When they ran, they took it with them. They stay just as sentimental and unrealistic as ever in their various new, safer, intellectual positions.

III 9   *New Yorker* W.H. Auden reviewing the Hart-Davis Oscar Wilde letters: ". . . since knowledge of an artist's private life never throws any significant light upon his work, there is no justification for intruding on his privacy." [This of course would seem to me absolutely true. But the absolute is always theoretical. Auden himself suggests that it applies to the writer (as Auden himself would say) *qua* writer. If, as well as a writer, he is a man convicted in a notorious case, his mistake in getting caught would seem to leave him no more right to be protected from public curiosity than any other man. A. concedes this: though principally I judge, because he is glad of what the letters or some of them do in exposing what a nasty bit of work Lord Alfred Douglas was. Yet it occurs to me that in cases like Wilde's (and one can feel quite sure; Somerset Maugham's, and Evelyn Waugh's) the private life—meaning: homosexual tendencies—may perhaps throw a very significant light on the obvious distaste, really the enmity, with which all three often present women in their work (In *Cakes & Ale*, the narrator takes 'Rosie's side: but it is always to spite other women). Yet, of course, a moment's reflection must make me reverse myself. If the reader's at all perceptive, the work in its plain bias, is telling him what 'knowledge' of the writer's private life could merely confirm. The 'significant light' is thrown on the work by the work. If a book is any good, it's good in itself: and what the author may have been like couldn't matter less.

III 26   If you're careless about money, you're of course a fool and are pretty likely to demonstrate the adage about being parted from it. But the observable fact remains that if you're careful about money it may keep you from being ruined, like the fool: but it

III 28   will also make sure you'll never be rich.

In such matters as food and drink, or even in the use of women, experience quickly teaches you not to be misled into imagining that because a little may be very good, more will be still better. The only case I can think of where this won't be true is (see above) that of money. There; a little is good, a lot *is* better.

IV 1   Morrow sent me *The Shoes of the Fisherman* by Morris A. West who seems to be an Australian, for some time a news-paper correspondent at the Vatican. This lets him tell you in very good journalese some interesting things about what it's like to be pope; though his fictional pope, and all his charac-ters, are a good deal less than real—without however being ridiculous or implausible—he is, I'd say, a kind of Pious Man's Nevil Schute. The Pontiff pronounced at one point in private conversation well enough handled technically, on S. Francis of Assisi "A man born out of his due time etc . . ." Idly, I was struck by the thought that this was an example of what might be called 'read-along'—you aren't thinking, you're just read-ing. That sounds all right: but wasn't S. Francis in fact a man born, if ever one was, in 'his due time'? A static church was making less and less provision for the sentimentalists who provided it with its energy. The end of the crusades had stopped up the needed outlets for zeal. The mass of practical people were treating (as they always did, would, and will) religious obligations like income tax return payments—it was simpler and easier to pay: and moreover, you got, even if you grum-bled, a sort of order. But the people who actually made 'reli-gion' viable were restless; they were bored; they needed some emotional fodder of an arresting kind. The Friars Minor pro-vided it—or, did *their* need provide the Friars Minor? At any rate, seen in retrospect at least, nothing could have been more timely than S. Francis.

IV 4   April *Show* (a magazine not to be around very long I think) has a story of John O'Hara's called *Yucca Knolls*. What it's about is the tough times hitting some Hollywood characters and you can't doubt that this is exactly the way it is today for a lot of people who rose in the movie industry when things were differ-ent. The detail doesn't matter: it's recognizably authentic, perfectly straight, perfectly honest and written with all com-petence. As usual, it raises what I can only call the Problem of John O'Hara. He has an excellent ear, a good eye, and there's never even a suggestion of that modern Norman-Mailer-type affectation, fakery, and sentimentality in its various dishonest disguises. Yet the truth is, too much of the time he leaves me, let's say, discontented. Even granting that he's right, every one really is a son of a bitch; and his demonstrations are nothing but truth, you (or I) keep feeling they aren't the whole truth. He tells you *what* as well as possible: but left out is, I suppose probably because it doesn't interest him; but possibly because some odd failure of insight keeps him from being able to see, the *why* which alone can make all this meaningful. The truth is somehow brought to be unconvincing. As a random example; Somerset Maugham's short stories, if occasionally trivial, are never in that sense unconvincing. In many of them there may be little meat (as contrasted with O'Hara's invariable good full measure) but it's digested. You don't fail to get your (even when minor) new acquist of true experience.

IV 5   *Six Studies in Quarreling Vincent Brome*. These are accounts of early-in-the century literary 'feuds' perhaps more instructively dealt with in Frank Swinnerton's amazing octagenarian *Death of a Highbrow* (by far the best book he ever wrote: and surely to write it at his age is quite a trick). The Chesterton and Belloc quarrels with people about catholic history have, of course, lost whatever importance or interest they might once have had: and it's hard to care what Jones thought of Shaw, or Shaw thought of anything: but H. G. Wells is quoted in a letter to Henry James (1915) "to you, literature is an end . . . to me, literature is a means. . ." (p. 99) and I can't help feeling this remains as good as new in explaining all honest differences between writers.

IV 10   If 'success' seems important to him, every born human being should surely be of good cheer. However handicapped, however incompetent, he's in the running. What, by common consent, constitutes 'success' can be had by absolutely anyone. You simply need luck: and luck never seems to have been at all concerned with any damned nonsense about merit. [but of course this only goes for good luck. Bad luck, as a matter of general experience, seems unerringly to find out lack of merit and go along with it.

IV 13   In a recorded radio statement, Bertrand Russell was heard suggesting that in the 'neucular situation' the most important step, if they weren't going to ban the bomb on his 'better red than dead' basis, for authorities to arrange to take now would be construction of a fall-out proof shelter perhaps at the south pole where relays of fertile young females should always be in residence along with a supply of stored frozen semen collected now before any more radioactive material was released for artificial insemination of them, so that the race, after its destruction in now inhabited countries, could be started over again.
[This irony may be a little labored; but I think I'd have to feel that if it came to that, the measure, if provident, would be

stupid. Why in God's name, you might surely ask, arrange to start such a race again? Let's just forget the whole business. [I'm sorry indeed to say that, in tape at least, Russell sounded definitely senile; that dreadful thing, the unconscious silly ass. If you're old, just keep quiet. (and maybe, if you're young, too]

IV 18   *New Yorker.* Edmund Wilson's extremely long '*My Fifty Years with Dictionaries and Grammars.*' What Wilson knows is as usual often interesting and often nicely put; yet most readers must have (meaning: I have) noticed a certain increasing creeping tediousness in his more recent writings. I had charged it once or twice to no great interest in what he happened to be writing about on my part. That wasn't true here, and I suddenly saw what was wrong. He used to confine himself admirably to a clear-phrased telling you only about those interesting things he knows; or, with generally good judgment, has set himself to dig up. Now, more and more, he interrupts to tell you things about Wilson—that '*My* Fifty Years' is the bad sign; though you'd never think of it and neither would he. The fact is, Wilson himself isn't interesting at all. He can pick out excellent stuff [*Patriotic Gore* was a wonderful job of judging what was good, but too little known] from other people's writing. Himself he cannot judge. The sad, ordinary, fact is something for all of us writing senior-citizens to bear in mind.

IV 22   The austerities practised were real and really remarkable, yet the unconcealable satisfaction they were giving him seemed to tell you the simple truth that self-denial can be one of the forms of self-indulgence.

V 1   Looking at Hortense Calisher's new book* I suddenly realized what it was that troubled me in what seems really to amount to the New Style in Serious Writing—I remember noting it as a more or less regular thing in Smith's 'Creative Writing' course kids last year. The exact or the specific is avoided as far as possible and by no means because sloppiness in writing or looseness in thinking makes the writer incapable of precise statement. There's an apparent feeling that exactness is narrow and confining and truth and life can't be fitted into it. There is a resulting resort to similie and generalization. Naturally, I think they couldn't be more mistaken. Nothing is really 'like' anything else. True propositions are all partitive—some men do or do not do so and so. As a reader, I want a writer to give me carefully and clearly facts intelligently observed. His comment on them is welcome if I see he has what seems to me sense; but I don't want him to mix them together because writers, even good ones, often don't have sense; and the disentangling job can be tiresome. A good example, I remember, was the late Mr.

Textures of Life (Boston: Little, Brown, 1963). Ed.

Hemingway. He could write, all right; but apparently he could not think.

V 8   What 'Modern Medical Science' can do to save the lives of people who are literally too young to die is impressive and surely good; but viewed realistically is it anything but a menace to people getting to the age when all they really have left to do is die? You're threatened with its vast resources for keeping you alive long after you ought to be dead. They'll be used if you give medical science a chance to use them. Mightn't a good deal be said for not giving it a chance? Don't have a 'check-up'. Don't let the 'condition' that, caught early on can be corrected, be caught. Let it do in its own way the work it was meant to do when it was meant to do it.

V 18   If at first you don't succeed, try, try again may be a good idea. But if at last you don't succeed—what then?

V 24   The simple statement must always be good writing. *The cat sat on the mat* can fairly be called perfect. Not a word wasted. No possible misunderstandings or confusion of meanings. But simplicity has also made the statement, in the strictest sense, insignificant. You've got simplicity; but at the expense of the specific and the precise. You've confined yourself to abstractions and so defeated the whole real purpose of writing. You've left out what the cat was like; what the mat was like; where the mat was; and why the cat's sitting on it was worth reporting at all. Simplicity not enough?

VI 1   *Wells (V 26) on Higginson:*[*] p. 221 H.'s 'Prelude' to his novel *Malbone* (1869) "One learns in growing older that no fiction can be so strange nor appear so improbable as the simple truth . . . For no man of middle age can dare trust himself to portray life in its full intensity, as he has studied or shared it; he must resolutely set aside as indescribable the things most worth describing, and must expect to be charged with exaggeration even when he tells the rest."
[the 'dare trust himself' and the 'resolutely set aside as indescribable' suggest in the phrasings that he has in mind the taboos of the time on the 'facts of life' and the difficulties of telling any real truth when the closest you can come to them and still get printed are those kinds of statement. But the 'no fiction can be so strange and improbable as the simple truth' comes down to saying: there is something wrong with the way I write. What makes 'simple truth' seem 'strange and improbable' must of course be its presentation. If a writer is gifted enough to 'portray life in its full intensity as he has studied or

---

[*]Anna Mary Wells, *Dear Preceptor: Life and Times of Thomas Wentworth Higginson* (Boston: Houghton Mifflin, 1963). Entry V26 comments on Emily Dickinson at Mt. Holyoke Female Seminary. Ed.

shared it' and what he portrays is or was true, he needn't worry: however strange, probability's implicit in it. When it isn't, that's for one reason only. Whatever he imagines, he hasn't managed to tell the 'simple truth'.

VI 3   *Wells-Higginson p. 229* Emily Dickinson quoted. "If I read a book and it makes my whole body so cold no fire can ever warm me I know *that* is poetry. If I feel physically as if the top of my head were torn off, I know *that* is poetry. These are the only way I know it. Is there any other way?"
[Even Dear Preceptor would probably see the question was strictly rhetorical. I've occasionally wondered about what might be called the Real Worth of Emily Dickinson. She seems, like William Blake, to labor her language with the word you couldn't possibly expect. This may have the virtue of never boring the reader with any same-old-stuff: but whether conscious or unconscious, it amounts to a formula. As long as it can keep you astonished, it works; but incessantly repeated it becomes, instead of astonishing, expected. Then you're likely to begin to look through the manner to the matter. Is, cockeyed words aside, anything to hold interest being said? Is any true experience rendered in an essential statement? Or is it just fancy work; the 'new' a little on the untrue side; the true a little on the twice-told side?

VI 20   *Diaries of George Washington Ed John Fitzpatrick H. Mifflin 1925* Over the last couple of weeks I've been getting thru these 4 volumes with great interest. I think the thing that must impress any reader most is constant evidence of a consistent and energetic good sense; and you must see that if he had made himself the richest man in the Colonies by the time of the revolution, it was through application and industry—he examined personally and knowledgably all his western lands; he 'rid' every day to all his Virginia plantations, observing in detail every bit of work that was going on and carefully considered how the smallest operation might be done better — that is: more quickly, more easily, and less expensively. You must also see, reading thousands upon thousands of his own words that meanness, penny-pinching, or greed for gain weren't remotely involved. What he aimed at was simply doing it right, eliminating irrational wastes. It's a tribute to him that you find yourself really set-down when it develops that the diaries stop somewhat before he took command of the continental army —|and all the more let-down when he resumes them (explaining that he had not before found time) in the last year of the war; because they are done with the same show of energetic good sense, sharp attention to detail, and simple businesslike perceptiveness. In some ways it's a sort of shock to see beyond any possible doubt that the inevitably more or less mummified figure of statues, coins, postage stamps, the suspiciously stuffed-shirt-like image of conventional history must actually, as a living man, have been every bit as good as, and maybe a little better than, the man of legend.

VI 27   Noting in the Washington Diaries (supra VI 20) that Washington was only 51 at the end of the revolution, I find myself, as I imagine many people do when they come to be nearly 60, feeling a sort of surprise to realize that I'm older than most of the historical figures whose image, if unconsidered, would be that of the boy's-eye-view still. My father, dead 43 years, died, I have to remind myself, 6 years younger than I am now. I know I am old: the figures certify it: but I begin to see that it's only the young or the very young who can see age as a state apart, the state of their masters & pastors, not seriously or convincingly to be conceived by them as ever young. Of course I know already that the grow-old-along-with-me stuff is eyewash and nonsense—it's the worst, not the best, that's sure as hell still to be; yet you can wonder, for example, if Our Lord Jesus Christ in legend supposed, as I remember, to have died at 33, really had enough experience in living to make his pronouncements as the gospels record them worth taking very seriously.

the incorrigible banalities of truth. What is true of you will be true of most men; what is true of most men will be true of you.

VII 4   Checking a point in *Aldous Huxley's Eyeless in Gaza* I came on a paragraph I remembered thinking of in connection with my note on Higginson (supra VI 1) p 397 ". . . the profound untruthfulness of even the best imaginative literature . . . almost total neglect of those small physiological events that decide whether day-to-day living shall have a pleasant or unpleasant tone. Excretion, for example, with its power to make or mar the day. Digestion. And, for the heroines of novel and drama, menstruation. Then the small illnesses—catarhh, rheumatism, headache, eyestrain . . . no mention of the part played by mere sensation in producing happiness. Hot bath, for example, taste of bacon, feel of fur, smell of freesias. In life, an empty cigarette case may cause more distress than the absence of a lover: never in books.' [the 'mere sensation' point seems quite untrue; books are full of that kind of thing: the empty cigarette case point on the other hand is good, but perhaps excusable because distress of that kind, however real, is hard for a reader to take seriously and the practised writer would instinctively reject detail he couldn't more surely control and direct. The passage goes on to mention "omission of the small distractions that fill the greater part of human lives" and again I can't imagine what makes H. think this. Novels have always been loaded with "reading the papers; looking into shops; exchanging gossip; with all the varieties of day-dreaming. . ." Recently, of course (H. is writing in 1936) all the 'physiological omissions' have been taken care of what comes to seem only too well. People don't go to the bathroom all day long in 'real life', and 'heroines' won't be menstruating much more than 1/6 of the time.

VII 12 M.M.* telephoned S. from Paris some back to ask if she'd be willing to handle the motion picture sale of her new book, which S. again for old times' sake said she'd do, and is doing (see above). Harcourt at once made copies of the book, to be published late next month, available. Called *The Group* it deals with some Vassar women of Mary's class of 1933 and as a novel is so far from good as to be a mess, reading like what it probably is, a salvaging and rather careless combining of shorter pieces meant for, but not taken by, the New Yorker. There are, of course, good short passages in it; and at least one long passage of such specific sexual detail—a minute-by-minute five page record of how to deflower a Vassar virgin with subsequent fingering of her until she comes again: and then an account of how a pesary is fitted to her (her ravisher's suggestion)—that popular interest seems probable. But I think for those reasons so infinitely mysterious that you can't even guess at them sensibly, the book is building-up to go and is going to be a great 'best seller'. Publishing Circles have that not to be defined 'something in the air' stir, S. discovers, getting on her 'handling' job. Fed with rumors, the movies are tumbling over themselves. Bill Jovanovich decided on a 1st printing of 75,000 (Mary has never sold anything to speak of, though probably no one has made herself (or himself) better known in Literary Circles). It will be very interesting to see—not, alas, that much will be learned, beyond the already known: nobody knows how the hell these things happen.

*Mary McCarthy. In the VII 10 entry Cozzens mentions that his wife was engaged in the movie deal for *The Group*. Ed.

VII 13 Another note on *The Group*. The Social Attitude. Mary's half-Jewish, half Irish background probably made her somewhat suspect socially in Vassar's 1933 eyes. Some young pinings or regrets probably intensify a covert yet evident intenser interest in the fashionable and rich than they can be said to warrant. This is an interest John O'Hara shows, or maybe the term is, betrays. Neither knew these people 'all their lives'; and each carefully and intelligently learned about them (though Mary in her St. George's Church scenes hasn't done her home work on the Episcopals). Probably (or perhaps) because Mary got to Vassar, while O'Hara did not get to college there's a dectable difference in underlying attitude. O'Hara doesn't learn about them because he wants to join them: he just wants to lick them. Mary's occasional cuts at them are spiritless, mere sour-grapes form. You can guess that in maybe unconscious female reverie, she's cleansed of her Jewishness and her Irishness and as of natural right joins them.

VII 16 That *The Group* (supra 12, 13) is becoming more and more a 'hot property' gets more and more evident. S. sensibly enlisted Harold Freedman to do what might be called the Leg Work on a split commission basis: and duly tipped off Ray Stark, who responded vigorously for free—in his case I gather you really do him a favor which is reward enough if Hollywood can know he has the inside track on such a 'property'. There is some suggestion that the commission S. & Harold might split could be on $500,000; and by all recent evidence this is not fantastic. I was interested to gather, perhaps a key to the nature of this kind of business, that neither Ray nor Harold, though asking for copies of the book, seemed to consider reading it necessary before they got to work selling it. You suspect that a 'hot property' may very well and very often change hands for consideration fairly to be called enormous without either actual seller or actual buyer ever having gone to the literally and truly irrelevant trouble of looking at it.

VII 20 Talbot Hamlin *Benjamin Henry Latrobe*. I've been reading this very good job for a week or so in snatches—a single criticism is the tiresome artlessness of mechanical management in the writing, repeated frequently: the pattern ". . . made him susceptible to offers of other employment, *as will appear*" (emphasis, as the law reports say, supplied). The trifling point is interesting. Mr. Hamlin seems almost constantly to feel that he may be confusing the reader; that he'd better explain, in the sense of warning the reader that this point is important. You may not see its importance now: but, later you will. The queer thing is that the thinking, the narrative order, isn't at all disorganized, requires no such anticipatory apologies for failing to put first things first. Why should a writer who isn't in the least inept so often use phrasings that are so much part and parcel of all inept writing?

VII 26 Looking up something that I thought I remembered Samuel Butler saying in *The Way of All Flesh*, I stumbled on (p. 355 et seq.) the description of Ernest 'successful' book "a series of semi-theological semi-social essays, purporting to have been written by six or seven different people, and viewing the same class of subjects from different standpoints. . ." [It is true that (supra VII 12) I'd been concluding from the Mary McCarthy business that nobody knows how the hell these things happen: and that Butler himself is shrewd and amusing on the general

subject of 'literary success'; and certainly there's nothing implausible in the situation as described and as of that time. But
even if there's no real sense in most 'success', then or now, you
have to see that something *has* changed. Just ask yourself
where a 'series' of such essays could get today; and you have to
see that vogues, fashions of the moment, are what may very
well count most, really account for, any more than minor
'success'.

VIII 8   Dismayed, you find the book's full of what oft was thought; yet
n'er, or nearly n'er, so ill-expressed.

VIII 12   the intense selfishness almost inseparable from self-sacrifice

7   20 August 1963-13 February 1964

VIII 24   I have a letter from a Mr. Applegate of the Syracuse University
library suggesting at length and in complimentary terms that
they would be in a position to preserve for posterity literary
materials of mine if I would honor them by depositing it with
them. It's true that I did just this at Princeton: but I reflect now,
as I reflected at that time, that I seem to be some kind of
exception among 'Authors';—and I simply could not care less
about a posthumous 'reputation'. By all accounts, this unconcern convicts me of a narrow and confined, rather than a wide,
ranging and universal 'spirit' (did Shakespeare feel indifferent?
The sonnets certainly say no. The idea of outlasting marble and
monuments seems to have been to him the most gratifying of all
his ideas). I suppose the truth is that subconsciously I come
about as close to absolute solipsism as a man can. When I end;
everything ends. I can see that thinking so is illogical; but like
everyone else, I feel first and think afterward. Clearly, what I
feel first is that the one reality is the 'me' of this moment. It
seems to give me the best evidence that I've ever seen adduced
that a subconscious mind does exist. You can't get at it, or
know about it in any rational sense; but *it* gets at, and knows
about the conscious you. Could intimations of this kind account for all 'religious' conviction?

VIII 25   More along what is surely the same line came to me on looking
over the uncertainties above. Like yearnings for fame, which, if
it came, could be nothing to you, yet still you think you want it;
like 'religious conviction' so clearly got from some feeling or
other that, no mater how nonsensical, this is true, there subsists
in me I can only guess equally psychopathic incapacity for
those 'poor me' feelings that seem almost universally normal.

S., for instance, though in every way of far 'stronger' character than I am, can be sincerely and whole-heartedly sorry for herself at the most minor crossing of any of her least hopes or wishes. This is feminine, you suspect: felt by women for no doubt good and adequate physical and psychological reasons seated in being female. But I have to see that the run of normal males feel it, too. I don't like having any wish or hope of mine crossed, either; but my temperamental reaction is to get sore, ill-tempered—or, in short, what I'd call in any one else, nasty. The concept of being unjustly used, unfairly treated, refuses to form. Whether it's deserved or not seems, to me, utterly irrelevant. I just want what I want when I want it. If I don't get it, that's bad luck, or bad management. I can't see that I'm reasonably entitled to any recourse against either.

VIII 28   Mary McCarthy's book (supra. v. 6) has been getting very good review treatment on the whole, and excellent 'space'. Unsurprisingly, there's some 'nasty' comment in almost all of them; and a lot in the Newsweek piece which was supposed to have been 'the cover story', unfortunately knocked out by the 'Freedom March', one judges. What made the 'nasty' cracks unsurprising was of course Mary's years of 'nasty' critical cracks about other writers, offered often with a wit that could really sting; and authors' sensibilities being what they usually are, you could safely bet she has plenty of unforgiving enemies. Still, considering the number of people she'd surely hurt and infuriated, I thought she was getting off okay. Certainly she wasn't getting anything like the kind of late-in-the-day venomous hatchet jobs the Jewish critics gave me (and indeed are still giving me); and I would have guessed that, as such a slashing critic herself, she'd be tough enough to give even less of a damn that I gave. [The damn I gave, and I must admit I gave it, was a first, really laughable, feeling of dismay: how could they seriously say what was so unfair and untrue? The right question of course would be: how could *I* seriously suppose someone who imagined I was holding him up to scorn would be either fair or truthful? Was I born yesterday?] I was, for this reason, astonished by S's evidently growing concern. She said Mary was going to be 'awfully upset'. I said: I'd think Mary could take care of herself if anyone ever could. S. said: Far from it: she broods over criticism more than anyone I ever worked with. This was indeed news to me: but I remember in idly pondering Dwight Macdonald's case—the paradox of a person whose solemn-ass humorlessness was utter editing a parody collection—I ventured the guess (supra V 6) that what he relished in parodies was his hope and belief that they were hurting, that the parodied author felt what, you could immediately guess further, *he* felt when he was made fun of. If you think the thing over, the truth does seem to be that those who're zealous and voluble in in dishing it out are never good at taking it. This might certainly suggest that the dishing-out comes to be done for the very reason that the disher-out can't take it. Anyone easily hurt is bound to have been hurt plenty in his or her process of growing up. Grown-up, there's a standing score to pay if, and whenever, you see your chance. But of course, in compensating yourself, you don't cure yourself. You're just as open as ever to being hurt more; so you will be; and so there's always a new score to be evened; so you'll even it any time you can. [of course, I can see the process, or part of it, myself. I'm no man of sensibility (and thanks, I'm sure, to nothing admirable—just some confidence of conceitedness) but though I wouldn't, as such men of sensibility always will, go even a little out of my way to pay my Jews back, if I could do it in passing, with no trouble, I have to admit that I now would and no doubt always will, act as I conveniently can to even my own little score. Nasty business: nasty people: and nothing to choose, really.

IX 1   If at first you don't succeed; fail, fail again.

The Anglican Digest prints a cut of 'the 1963 summer book mark,' at thirty five cents a packet of 25. It's text is that First and Great Commandment; and seeing it isolated that way in fancy letters, I found myself suddenly moved to reflect that the idea was really idiotic. Even given such very fortunate situations as my own, it's hard to figure out just why thou shalt love the Lord thy God with all thy heart and with all thy soul and with all thy mind, unless your line of thought is: screw you (or them) Jack; I've got mine. If you look around you, conceiving the Lord thy God to be really in charge, it may be okay to fear Him; but to hell with loving Him. Obviously, you can't trust Him an inch; and He's about as mean and heartless a bastard as anyone ever saw or heard of. (Well, of course, nobody ever really did see Him).

IX 3   He's the kind of person you expect at any moment to go Catholic.

IX 5   The *New Yorker* carries a Naomi Bliven review of the second volume of Edel's *Henry James*, from which I learn something I for some reason (maybe, relative indifference) never knew. The review remarks: ". . . James set out to do something unprecedented in American letters — to be a self-supporting full-time writer. . . in 1870 he had been earning money as a writer for 6 years. . . in England where the cost of living was lower, James could live, though modestly, if he wrote steadily. He did; and his work always found a market in magazines. . . he made a living, never a surplus. . ." [This interested me; because it might possibly explain a quality in HJ's work that has always made me like it less than current criticism says you should. As in the case of Sinclair Lewis, the old SEP tripe writer suddenly taken seriously, the twig was bent. You learn habits of journalism, of getting on with the job, competently turning out the hack-work without wasting time considering or reconsidering. I'd say this came naturally to Lewis: but in James' case, it didn't; and when he could, he reacted all too strongly, treating himself consciously or unconsciously to over-consideration once he could afford to. Yet habits formed early are strong; and in the midst of the over-consideration you're disconcerted to find 'journalism' breaking out. [I speak of course for no one but myself.

The kind of sincere dishonesty of a man who has been hurt and is angry. The witness that he bears is false; but you can't fairly call him a liar. For his emotion's vengeful reasons, he so much wants bad things to be true about the person who hurt him, that they become true. He is being quite honest about them.

IX 14   *TLS* In a review of a Bibliography of D. H. Lawrence by one Warren Roberts under the caption 'Lawrentiana' one gets dismaying glimpses of these industries of the 'James Joyce Scholarship' type. The reviewer takes Mr. Roberts sharply and seriously to task for a good many 'inaccuracies ("Prof. Roberts records that *Apocalypse* was translated into Japanese five years before Lawrence wrote it"). All this has obviously no possible relation to 'literature'. The solemn and voluminous labor simply proceeds in a vacuum with an actual accomplishment, if you stand off at look at it disinterestedly; *out of the mountain, the ridiculus mouse*. While both Joyce and Lawrence remain 'hot' critical properties, all right; and 'liberal' college required-reading can maintain sales to a degree; I must wonder just how many copies are sold to adult readers who want them because they find the contents rewarding; and who really read all the way through, nowadays, anything by either.

IX 22   October *Harper's* has a large hunk of a forthcoming book by Vincent Sheean called painfully: *The Tangled Romance of Sinclair Lewis and Dorothy Thompson* in which the only new material seems to be Sheean's introduction of himself as considerably closer to both than either Mark Shorer's exhaustive work, on internal evidence here, would seem to show he had been. The old material continues as before to suggest that they were, in their different ways, both pretty awful people—always posing, always acting, always insatiable in their appetite for recognition and renown. All that's so far been told me doesn't make me want to hear or know much more about either of them. Yet, while this certainly goes for Lewis, who is seen to

have been a sophomore all his life, concerned with nothing so ·
much as over-compensating himself for neglects shown him by
Yale when he *was* a sophomore there; I I must admit I'd be a
little interested to know how Dorothy came to be 27 before she
married; and why, then, it was to that previous Austrian husband.

IX 23   More on the Splendors & Miseries of being a Writer. *News-*
week reviewing *My Brother Bill* by John Faulkner quotes from
the text: "Bill could not stand the hurt of adverse criticism. He
simply refused to hear it. Except on rare occasions he wouldn't
even talk to anyone about his writing. He was simply protect-
ing himself from hurt. When I started writing he told me never
to read a review. He did not explain why. I know now. [I think
there may be another explanation for not talking about your
writing (I *would* think so). It may go to the enigmatic matter of
Mark: 5.30: *Who touched my clothes?* You feel, or know, that,
that way, the virtue (i.e. efficacy) can go out of you.
[About the 'hurt' of adverse criticism, it's true that I admitted
and must go on admitting supra IX 10)* that when I got my
spattering of spleen and venom from the Jewish critics I was
flabbergasted; and really have to back-down a little on my
years-old claim that you ought always to read 'adverse criticism'. Certainly, in that stuff there was nothing useful or instructive; reading it was a waste of time. Still reading it, I wasn't
in any way 'hurt': I was only angered. Of course, this may
amount to the same thing; in that you do feel, and you'll
probably (even certainly) show, when you can, your resentment by running down those who have run you down. That's
of course, if, when the chance comes, you're still able to care. I
know me. Unlike Brother Bill, I won't care.

*From IX 10: "Of course it's only right for me to note further that my view,
however factually just, is certainly colored with a little bit of ill-feeling that
wouldn't have been there before the Jewish critics' attacks on me. If it remains
'a little bit' only, I need to remember this is due to relative indifference on my
part, not to my higher regard for 'fairness' or 'honesty.' " Ed.

IX 28   More on Splendors & Miseries etc (supra IX 23) In a *News-*
week review of published correspondence of Robert Frost the
passing comment is made that when he became old he quar-
reled with several former literary friends because he felt they
had not done all they could to get him a Nobel Prize. My first
thought was that here, clearly, is a symptom of senility. I don't
mean that my own instinct, which would make me do almost
anything, if it could be done inconspicuously, to *avoid* getting a
Nobel Prize is right or normal or due to anything but some
self-conscious and surely psychopathic (I wouldn't be at all
surprised if a psychiatrist could show me that my real complaint is that I'm so vain or conceited subconsciously that I

became miffed at not getting it on the strength of my first book) aversion to mechanical fan-fare (more of the same, no doubt. I don't really object to fanfare: I just want more of it than a prize could get me, if I only knew?). But I do mean that I don't (as usual) see how one could let oneself importune people to do what they'd shown they weren't inclined to do for you. To be any good, any satisfaction, 'honors' would seem to me to have to come to you, not be gone after or wangled for.

But perhaps you need to consider what must have been Frost's special case. He might, and you can see why he might, badly need a sort of justification by prize. Writers being writers, it's easy to imagine the years and years of hardly being able to stand it F. could have spent while all attention, in poetry, went to people like T. S. Eliot or Ezra Pound: and doubtless even worse, to almost every small-fry imitator of them.

X 18   *Readers Subscription* offering quote. "The chance to explore the wonders of *Finnegans Wake* is one of the few great intellectual and esthetic treats that these years have yielded" Edmund Wilson
[No comment seems possible. Except, perhaps: yield, years, yield; Wilson (Edmund) is treating us.

X 26   Harcourt has been sending S. the Mary McCarthy reviews so I saw in the new (and I'm sure transient) *The New York Review of Books* the leading, venomous, and abnormally long and wordy attack on her by Norman Mailer (One's first impulse was to wire in: Stop; wait; look, boys, she's half Jewish herself. Benefit of Clergy, you know;) but you have to see that the real point is the one that's so obvious you have trouble accepting it: she is selling a lot and looks like selling more and the unsuccessful novelist-turned critic (Mr. Mailer's only, and far less deserved, success was an accident of long ago) just can't stand it. The one point of slight interest is the illustration of that standard tactic of effective polemics. When you want to run down a book or a writer you waste no time attacking weak points (*The Group*, one has to admit, is full of them. What you go for are the strong points, the things plainly good. These, you assert flatly, are absent or lacking. Surely this is risky; since any intelligent reader can see they aren't absent, they aren't lacking? No. This is the Big Lie technique; and, at any given moment, it's apt to be irresistible; because the natural reaction of the human mind is a perhaps shocked but still ready feeling that, because of its extent and completeness, this untruth surely might or even must be true—otherwise, how could anyone be crazy enough to advance it?

X 28   More Criticism. *Sat. Review* 26 *Oct* Winfield Townley Scott. 'Poetry Quarterly': "Take the haphazards of any three months' production of new books of poetry, and if the quality is not amazingly high—and it is not—one is still amazed at the quantity." [and, I would add, at the asked retail prices: one volume here is $5.75, one $6. I suppose it may be sensibly argued that since almost no one is going to buy it anyway the price hardly matters: but that point of quantity is interesting because as nearly as I can judge the only people who read any new poetry are other poets and with them it seems to be a critical exercise, mostly in technical disagreement. Scott: "What we have in ———— 's verse is the seamless style, the lovely rhyming, the beautifully's modulated stanzas, and the literary allusions of the 19th century romantics. It is all very able; and. . . we fail to question how much it emanates, as poetry should, from our own time. . ." [This surely odd dominant idea today that poetry can't be good in itself, in mere moving or effective arrangement of words, but is 'good' in reference to something else, in say, 'emanating from our own time' defeats me, and also, I naturally think, defeats today's poetry. Shakespeare's sonnets sure as hell don't emanate from our own time: and, if you aren't familiar with his times' obsolete language, are frequently unclear: but if you take that small trouble, they're surely as superlatively, staggeringly good now as they ever were. Scott comments: "When this (the seamless style etc) occurs in our own country most critics scream in anguish "Robert Hillyer!" And they are correct though I persist in believing they sometimes underestimate lyrics, Hillyer's and others, that would be flawless in any era." [The phrasing however suggests that Mr. S. is merely working both sides of the street. Still, that he dares to say any such thing might suggest a vogue changing, an era ending. And high time, too.

X 31   *Still More Lit. Crit* John Simon (in a collection: *The Acid Test*). On the late James Agee: "There is one more thing: Agee could write. 'The Big Sleep is a violent, smoky cocktail which puts you along with the cast, into a state of semi-amnesia through which tough action and reaction drum with something of the nonsensical solace of a hard rain on a tin roof'. Note how image flows from, reinforces, and tops image, and how the whole is greater than the sum of its parts—as in the best poetry." [Note, too, the affected, inexact phrasing, the irrelevant references and general emptiness of meaning as 'image flows from etc'. What goes on here? The writing is, relatively, lousy: why do a few of these Critical Queers find it in their interest to assert that it's GREAT? This matter of motive in criticism (what's in it for the critic) might be worth some study.

XI 2   Those psychiatric cases, once with awe, called mystics.

XI 8   *TLS.* C. P. Snow, in the course of a long, temperate reply to the

F. R. Leavis abuse of him, called: *The Two Cultures: A Second Look*, impressed me with a show of perception and intelligence both sober, and, astonishingly, humorous, which I'll admit neither novels of his I've read, nor the one occasion I met and listened to him (at dinner at Cass Canfield's some six years ago) had led me to expect. I'm speaking of the 'tone' of the piece and its management, the content being of necessity the words-words-words that any dissertation on anything like 'culture', by very definition, must be. In connection with the attacks on him, I was surprised and amused to have him touch in passing a point I'd wondered about in attacks made on me. "Do certain kinds of animosity lead to an inability to perform the physical act of reading?" He goes on to give an example: the ascription to him of the statement: We die alone. It was true that the text said what might amount to the same thing: Each of us dies alone; and he wasn't quibbling about meaning. Simply; why the odd little inexactness? It seemed indeed to suggest that Leavis himself, in that anger of what really must boil down to envy, (cf supra X 26 Mailer vs. McCarthy) could not bring himself to read with care; and that those who supported L, repeating the 'quote', read only Leavis, never troubled to read the text at all. [From my own experience, the suggested 'inability to read' can easily go beyond mere not getting right something you did say. It can say you said, and abuse you for saying things, specifically quoted, which were never, not in any form, in the text at all. Obviously the quoter is 'sure' he saw it there—anger might naturally make him stupid in many matters of judgment: but anger's self-interest would if it could surely take great care to avoid the kind of mistake that even anger would have to see must fatally cripple anger's whole attempt. The explanation almost has to be a kind of 'blacking-out'; a stupidity of unseeing—what must have been meant by 'Dummheit' in Schiller's celebrated line.

XII 2   I've been looking at Edmund Fuller's new novel, *The Corridor* with (I fear) the faint hope that I could find grounds to drop him a 'Nice Note' which of course could be and would be expected to incline him to disagree with the Jew-boy line about me in his frequent critical pronouncements. That in a dirty game you'd better stop giving yourself airs and play it their way is of course only common sense: but I like such exercises of common sense so little, it really relieved me to find no grounds for any note were given, the book being almost a model of ineptitude. So much so that it reminded me of a notion I've had about a 'writing course' which would base itself on examples of what not to do. Here, for example, the mishandling of the 'throw-back' is demonstrated with such clarity and completeness that no 'student' of 'creative writing' could fail to see the important technical point. Our author has his man allowed to sleep at the hospital, not knowing whether his wife will live until morning. Action is suspended: the reader, understandably, prepares to wait. The night is duly got through, partly used for an ineffectively handled and uninformative dream of the man's. His wife has not died: and now, come morning, when direct present action had no excuse for not being resumed, our author halts it with a jerk and wants the reader to listen to a lengthy account of what happened once. In one way this is a mere mechanical detail; matter will indeed always be more important than manner; but in a novel, in narrative presentation, manner often will be matter. That night, wasted technically, that morning made a stumbling block — no; when that's the matter, the matter doesn't matter.

XII 4   Understanding All & Forgiving All Etc. It's true that if you have average intelligence (I suppose everyone using that term means by it: intelligence less than his own) even a superficial study of people generally lets you see why they think as they think and so have to do as they do. Once you understand that, the silliness of blaming them for what they can't possibly help may pretty well stop you if you wish to act reasonably. What you're exhorted to is: Sit there: don't just do something! Still, you can't let yourself be stultified this way. The bear that would have bit you may not be reasonably blameable: but if you have a gun, in reason you no more than even matters if you shoot him first.

XII 7   The Hudson Vitamin Co's catalog lists among incidental 'reliable drug products' something called *Smokurb* to take advantage of current agitation on the matter with what I gather is a lobeline tablet supposed to making stopping easy. While saying it's up to you they point out that 'smoking never did you any good'. Like most other long-time smokers I'm inclined to go along with the sentiment. It's indeed a senseless habit and when you remember that, to start, it was really disagreeable, something you had to learn to do—well! But isn't this just a little thoughtless; or: how ungrateful can you get? With one kind of satisfaction or gratification or another you've been lighting cigarettes for forty years. When things weren't too good, you got a timely relief or comfort: when things were good, the good seemed somehow enhanced. Even if it were claimed that this was all imagination, that can't change the experience. What you imagine to be true *is* true for you. To say it's silly to start, or even to wish you could kick the habit is all very well; but to say it never did you any good is stupid and untruthful.

XII 14   Southern Climes Etc. It would seem only right and reasonable to go away for awhile this winter; but I must admit I feel no real

wish to and this is for the one simple and only reason that I
can't imagine what I'd do to put in the time until I got back. It's
true that nice weather would be nice: but after all, in my study I
have nice weather no matter what it's doing outside: and here I
never seem to have any trouble passing the time. I'm not
interested in any resort 'recreations': I don't want to meet
people I don't know and here, of course, I'm helped by the fact
that S., I've never been quite sure whether consciously or just
unconsciously, doesn't want me to, either. She probably 'has a
feeling' that in an uprooted state, I might get out of hand from
her standpoint, leaving her in the lurch while I drank with men
and fooled with women; and indeed I don't know that this isn't
smart of her rather than silly of her. If that's so, and I'm
virtually sure it's so; because, you could see after some private
pondering, she decided against the special West Indies cruise
(I'd put a deposit on it, figuring that something simple and
definitely 'un-gala' of the kind might get me through. I'd have a
base on board; and the ship would move me to some new island
of the less frequented sort every day, which would occupy me at
least tolerably in noting its 'charms' weren't up to much), the
dilemma must really exercise her. Her preferred solution would
be to find and buy a small place in some more or less deserted
part of Florida where a second study in which I could be
counted on contentedly to occupy myself by myself might be
fitted up; and, outside, it wouldn't be snowing (at least, not
often). Alas, the stuff, she must see, dreams are made on. We
haven't that kind of money; and while nothing would delight
her more than to get rid of Shadowbrook, haste makes waste. I
mustn't be taken out of here until some other place, at least as
safe, to put me in is found. I have to feel complimented by the
concern; even though recognizing what the Object of the Af-
fections of all of us must actually be.

XII 15 Those 'canvassers' of the 'civil rights committee' (supra XI 30)*
got around to me this afternoon. A young male and a young
female drove in and you had to note that, perhaps melancholy,
fact that they looked exactly as you would expect—meagre
would be the shortest way of putting it: the male skinny and
homely with bigrimmed glasses; the female plain, sharp featured and sallow—they didn't appear to be married to each
other, though it would have made a good match, I couldn't help
feeling. Perhaps because I'd been annoyed a little by some
smugnesses of Sumner Kean, the *Berkshire Eagle's North
Berkshire Weekly* correspondent in his piece yesterday over the
fact that, last week 'the household head of 275 out of 515
visited signed the pledge. Only 83 actually refused, and 160

*Cozzens's note on the refusal of a Williams College employee to accommo-
date Negro girls in her home.

were not at home' I decided I'd make an 84th even though I'm
not insensible to a certain disarming pathos in such
Earnestness—is it their fault that they aren't attractive, confi-
dent, and amusing? So I said that though I had no objection to
having anyone, regardless of color, creed, or inferiority complex, who could afford the Williamstown tax rates for a
neighbor, I thought it impudent to solicit pledges to obey what
was now, wisely or foolishly, the law; and that the social and
economic coercion being applied to those who might not be of
my opinion in the matter and who definitely were not in my
position of perfect freedom to tell anyone I liked to go to hell,
would never get any support from me. They were a good deal
flustered: and I must, and I do, remind myself that I seem to be
in increasing danger of turning into an Irascible Old Man.

XII 20   Mary McCarthy, still first on the best sellers lists, I was interested to learn from S., has decided, as I finally had to, that
the truth—hesitate to believe it though I did (and she, I gather,
did) because it seems too simple: really, too childish, or at least,
too puerile—about critical gang-ups by the 'liberal' mostly
Jewish 'intellectual' critics are provoked by best-selling and
nothing but best-selling. Any book that sells a lot, and yet has
to be recognized as 'serious' writing, not tripe, not 'popular',
has to be No Good. These 'critics' are book-writers themselves;
but their books don't sell. Merit, it follows, can have nothing to
do with sales: quite the contrary. It must be merit that prevents
sales; or at least, they'll never say different. [Granted a touch of
rationalizing, MM licking some wounds: the point seemed
perhaps borne out in a fine ironic way by the fact that MM,
plainly provoked by the TIME cover story on J.D. Salinger,
could stand his 'success' no better than the rest of the gang and
took him apart, never, one guesses, dreaming that before the
year was out, the crazy chances in this business would put her
in his position, the intolerable commander of attention and
sales which had never been hers. [I will have to say that her
'strictures,' whatever their motive, seemed to me relatively
reasonable. S's phony and maudlin qualities made me write
him off on his first book as something for sophomores. But if
there hadn't been so many sophomores, and so many vocal
ones, more and more of them outside little-mag. circles, I'd bet
a lot she'd never have found a thing amiss—or at any rate,
never have found a need to speak out about it.

XII 28   John O'Hara's *The Hat on the Bed* which (my God) must be his
third published book this year, presents a short story collection. All the stuff has the honest qualities of people seen clearly
and reported with definitely gifted care and this is good (who
does better?) yet the problem persists. What can his experience
have been? My own experience (of about the same length as

his) has been that 'people' by and large are, as I think Somerset Maugham once said, generally not too bright but generally they have their hearts in the Right Place. O'Hara's procession, literally unbroken, of mean & cheap bastards, all quite convincing and also all wonderfully varied in situation and character is hard for me (for my experience) to accept and credit. It's my experience, so constant that occasional exceptions almost shock me, that if you're honest with a person, he'll be honest right back: that if you're civil and decent in your dealings with him, he'll be the same: that if you need help, most people will, if they possibly can, try to help you. In short, I don't remember ever in my life meeting personally a character of O'Hara's. And yet, as I say, they are so presented that they're perfectly real. I can't for a moment doubt that they do exist, and do behave exactly as he reports.

XII 29   *Note on above.* It occurs to me that what I describe as 'my experience' isn't any absolute observation of life; it's no more than my temperament's view of things and people as they affect me personally. Coloring or conditioning that 'view' may be that (for whatever psychological reasons) I've never wanted much of anything from anyone—except, perhaps, to be left or let alone. I can see that this is abnormal; and what amounts to a defect in me. But if your temperament's such that you *do* want things from other people, you no doubt feel differently toward them. Whether you get the things you want may not be of first importance, either. That is: even supposing you do get them, the fact that you *had* wanted them, that your desires had reduced you to wanting them, made you try to get them, could perhaps leave you as resentful as if you hadn't got them.

XII 31   It seems to be the simple perhaps sad fact that our human nature makes it apparently impossible for anyone to really love anyone else. This is an extension of the ruminations above; but not, I think, going contrary to them. It's not you who's loved. What your professed lover loves is all too evidently the enjoyment, the good, the use he or she finds you are, or thinks you could be, to him or her. Of course, there's this about it. The feeling's never faked or phony. That's a love that's forever true. And certainly all any human being can be entitled to; since he or she isn't going to be able to return anything different or 'better.' Here, that temperament that 'wants' may have its real trouble. If you want some one to love you for yourself, not for herself or himself, you're crying for the moon—a real expense of spirit in a waste of shame.

I 2   Off and on I've been getting through *Frank Harris' My Life and Loves* which for some reason I never happened to see back in the days when it 'suppression' made it regarded as a treasure of

pornography perhaps second only to Fanny Hill. As in the case
of Henry Miller, that side of it seems unjustly or unfairly delt
with by what I guess you could call Fate. When finally published openly, the 'shock value' and so commercial value that
was in it back when it was written has been almost totally
dissipated. Then, a certain amount of the material had really
never been seen in print before; now, all of it has been seen in
print dozens of times. This leaves the reader unlikely to be
moved by considerations which would have (and did; a dozen
mediocre books were vested with unreal and even ridiculous
importance for no other reason) forty years ago singled it out
for its Honesty & Candor in the recurring sexual detail. Today,
I'd think the thing likely to strike most grown-up readers could
hardly be any factitious 'honesty' of that kind. Quite the opposite. What it smacks of is simple and inveterate dishonesty. This
seems to be a cumulative effect. There's a false-sounding turn
of phrase here, an unconvincing detail there. One by one, each
could be no more than inept phrasing: but the incidence is so
great that you soon reserve judgment: and then feel stronger
and stronger doubt; and then just *know* he's lying. That is: as
you read about his acquaintance with the Great (meaning the
Notable) and really according to him, all the Great of the day,
you soon find yourself wondering a little whether a good many
of them, especially among those who were dead when he wrote,
would be astonished to learn how greatly he was admired by
them and how much he influenced them. An example would be
the case of Boulanger in Paris. He tells how he told B. just what
to do. B., it seems listened respectfully to the little English
journalist's advices; but alas for B, he didn't have the courage
and clarity of vision of a Frank Harris and so didn't do it. That
finished the general: and certainly it's not to be denied that the
general *was* finished shortly.

I 12   In the very shaky looking *New York Review of Books* V. I no.
11, a Marvin Mudrick (could he be kidding?) takes apart
Arthur Mizener's *The Sense of Life in the Modern Novel*. MM
had a chief fault to find with Mizener's (I can hardly believe it)
good words about me. I'd gather Mizener was using me as any
stick to beat some dogs: but 'Marvin' gives a demonstration of
the S.O.P. in the Jewish Cozzens-delendus-est campaign that is
so good, so exactly typical, I thought it worth noting.
"[Mizener] quotes . . . from Cozzens on responsibility: 'his thin
strong fingers, nervous but steadily controlled pressing' Col-
onel Ross's arm, he says 'I'll do the best I can, Judge: and you
do the best you can: and who's going to do it better?' A
predilection for upper-class platitudes or spongily heroic
stances is neither Trollopean nor otherwise entertaining."
The first thing you notice is the quite skillful lifting out of

context of the quoted phrases, both the descriptive one and the fragment of dialogue. I don't know what Mizener supplied: but I think it would probably have to have been the whole paragraph or passage as printed. That wouldn't serve 'Marvin'. Anyone able to read at all would almost have to see that the platitude wasn't 'upper-class' (the popping out of such terms is the real give-away: you're let in on what actually activates the dim critical view. A Jewish boy finds or fears he's more likely to be a private than an officer: so officers are no good, and neither is the army) but strictly Military. Platitudes truly 'upper class' would all be cynical or sceptical, not simple-mindedly frank & earnest. In the same way, if you were allowed to read the whole passage you'd have to see that 'spongily heroic' (that really awful use of words might I think be significant: practice to deceive may lead to some instinctive avoidance of the exact and explicit. False matter must always make for a false manner?) is, supposing it to be meant to mean: affected, high-falutin or unreal, just what the 'stance' unmistakably couldn't be. A simple (if you like) temperament and a limited (if you like) intelligence is being just as sincere as hell.

I 14   A last thought (and, no new one) on the above. Because of what is no doubt a simple temperament of my own (and, indeed, a limited intelligence: since its limits irk and thwart me daily, telling myself they aren't there just wouldn't work) I'm no good at bearing grudges. I know perfectly well this has nothing to do with a magnanimity that might be admirable; it's just a weak want of perseverance. Just, I suppose, as celerity is never more admired than by the negligent, the persistence of this Jewish 'hate', its energy in falsification, its richness of invention and resource, awes me at least a little. I think the point comes out clearest when I reflect that most of what they like and admire seems to me genuinely bad. While of course I don't think it is, I have no trouble conceding faults of taste and judgment in me make me think that; and certainly nothing impells me to show or prove that I am right. What's got into you when you're impelled to work hard, to study ways to tamper with evidence, to go on and on with a project which can't make you a nickle and may even (the fact seems to be) discredit and hurt you?

I 18   *TLS letter* (in the now infinitely boring controversy over *The Naked Lunch**—at least the correspondence has done me the service of assuring me there can be no possible reason to read the book) "Doctor Johnson, though baited as much as his contemporaries (and in less respectful ways than via your columns) still fairly pointed out that 'he that writes may be considered as a kind of general challenger, whom everyone has

*By William Burroughs. Ed.

the right to attack'; and that 'to commence author is to claim praise: and no man can aspire to honour but at the hazzard of disgrace.' "
[By God, I must admit the Doctor had something there in that 'to commence author'; and I ought to, and I hope will, stop griping about the Jew-boys.

I 25 More on 'Sex Mores'. TIME also developed the point that the virtual end of 'censorship' in the last few years (I remember a year or so ago, in connection with the magazine EROS, feeling active concern about this seeing how 'far' you could go and the jeopardy in which they'd put the hard-won right to write honestly if they tried to print, specifically, *Fanny Hill*. *Fanny Hill* is today on every bookstand) would seem naturally associated with 'laxity' in sexual behaviour. This would look likely; but the timing in itself suggests that 'laxity' causes pornography, not pornography, 'laxity'. Indeed, I wonder if the 'laxity' hasn't dealt pornography quite a blow just as it may be dealing itself quite a blow. When you couldn't speak of, could only think of a cunt, when couldn't properly see, let alone a cunt, even an ankle, 'sex' was obviously far more exciting and interesting. I don't mean that speaking of and seeing cunts is apt to make them go out of use or favor—but, after all, the pleasure *is* brief, the position *is* ridiculous; and anything that worked to gloss these blunt truths, like secrecy and strangeness, were surely aids to desire and elements of enjoyment—the mons veneris, a kind of captain jewel. The point's not one likely to be reasoned out: but I'd expect an unconscious recognition of it will, along with the human need to pamper one's ego, to be not-as-other-men, work before long a reaction, really a change in fashion. 'Purity' will start to become the thing; while lapses from it will again take on an excitement now at least partly lost.

I 29 Some thought-provoking by the *New York Review of Books*. On what seems most accurately described as the Sophomore Circuit ridden by most 'little' reviews and most 'liberal' critics the pretentious, the obscure, and the odd-ball are, of their very nature and by definition, inevitably and always the literary thing. I suspect that being the Thing is what makes feasible the extremely lengthy and labored 'criticism' of them—that's not read by anyone. Its mass simply indicates what the present Thing is. The grown-up reader, not interested in that, isn't likely to be talked out of his finding that one John O'Hara is worth, any day, a dozen Norman Mailers.

I 30 When you get older—and I recognize that I should stop saying 'older'; old is the word—there can be something a little disturbing about what surely ought to be Fond Recollection's show of proof that your luck has been so consistently good as to be almost beyond belief. I must see in my own case that this was always truest when it was most undeserved, when stupid or wanton behaviour of mine got me into fixes (and not all youthful) where bad trouble would seem in right and reason inescapable. But, every time, I escaped; and by no means, not ever, thanks to any resource of my own. So far, so good; all right; but the observations of, say, five decades of reasonable ability to observe must suggest to you that our human life just isn't, just can't be, all like that; and, not without trepidation, you must suspect that when the evening-up comes, necessarily not too long from now, it will be a lu-lu.

8   16 February 1964-20 October 1964

II 18   Demonstrably, the most dangerous thing anyone can ever do is to be born. You're making a contract, with no escape clause to die at the pleasure of the nature of things. Why do this?

II 21   Resuming a reading through of *Thoreau's Journals* in a new Dover 14 vols in 2 reprint that I got hold of I was amused to find I had in a special sense lost my place; and found myself getting a little restive over passages like (new paging: 57): "The true laborer is recompensed by his labor, not by his employer. Industry is its own wages. Let us not suffer our hands to loose one jot of their handiness by looking behind to a mean recompense, knowing that our true endeavor cannot be thwarted, nor we cheated of our earnings unless by not earning them." You seem to see here, if you look carefully, glibness, not seasoned reflection. In many ways, 'industry' particularly of his and my kind is indeed its own wages: but I'd like to see the evidence that proves 'true endeavor cannot be thwarted' (unless of course you test for 'true' by noting whether or not it *is* thwarted) or that not getting earnings proves a man didn't earn them. Reading along with small running dissents of this kind, and indeed wondering if reading him (in part) 40 years ago I hadn't formed too favorable an opinion, I came on one of the marginal notes dating the entries, and so was reminded that when he wrote the passages making me restive he was 23; and, *that* considered, far from doing badly, he was doing damn well.

II 27   *TLS* has a 13 Feb. piece that overcomes (and how easily) resolves I make to note no more the stupid and tedious plugs and back-bitings of our literary criticism. In a middle article a couple of American volumes of criticism are considered pretty much de haut en bas. One: Chester E. Eisinger. *Fiction of the*

Forties. U. of Chicago. The anonymous writer of the middle
interested me with turns of phrase that I couldn't help suspect-
ing showed him to be an American; and surely one of my poor
Jew-Boys; and even perhaps that poorest of those poor, my
sore-as-a-pup, Dwight Macdonald. (I think it was William
Buckley who told me TLS had a connection with him; and now,
itself, mostly Jewish direction, operating along *Commentary*
lines). At any rate, there's a wonderful passage that goes: "In
general, though, the professor [Eisinger] is a great labeller, and
for him it is satisfying to say that James Gould Cozzens is 'the
Pennsylvania Voice of Aggressive Aristocracy' or Wright Morris 'the Artist in Search of America'. What is the artistic value of
their novels? It would not be true to say that such a question is
disregarded, but the sharp and justified criticism Professor
Eisinger eventually makes of Cozzens does not stop him giving
more than twenty pages to Cozzens' work." [Cozzens delendus
est—not so?

[Still, indirectly and unintentionally you're given some idea of
'your reviewer's' evident ideas of 'artistic value'. You can guess
this has no connection with any presentation of true experience, of people as they are and life as it is. All you need to
determine is (never minding the matter) how close the manner
comes to fashions of the moment in the recherché phoney.
Minding the matter, artistic lapses are even more evident.
Characters are neither startlingly poor nor strikingly vicious.
There is a derth of Feeling (gross unsentimentality). The
thinking is clear and simple, to be understood by any fool.
Everything said is too explicit to require expounding. Artistic
value it has nix. What has artistic value is lynching of negroes;
how poor Jews make a living or don't; and the woes of
homosexuals or narcotic addicts. [there's also that Voice of
Aggressive Aristocracy point of the good professor's. I suppose
what you really get there is an instructive glimpse of the under-
dog's eye-view. He's figuring how *he* would feel and act if *he*
were top dog, in that modest sense. Naturally, he can't understand the normal attitudes of people who have no account to
square, nobody to get back at, and no need or wish to impress
anyone.

III 1   Those same good resolutions I'm afraid I find collapsing again
in the face of the vast N.Y. fuss over the Rolf Hochhuth *The
Deputy* show: and I'm afraid it would be a lie if I denied that it
pretty well fills me with that: O 'tis Sport feeling of Hamlet's.
Far from displeased, I must wonder if Jewish over-confidence,
grown bigger than its boots in making free to go out and get
solitary protestant gentiles like me who are thought remiss in
the now wanted ass-kissing, hasn't gone to the Jewish head, or
at least the Intellectual Jewish head. Of course I'm not going to

comply with the requirement; but just not complying is all I'll
bother to do. It isn't all the Catholics will bother to do. What's
being taken on here is something in their own image. Here
they're up against a similar, really ethnic, chattering with rage,
gnashing of teeth, and dirty, no-holds-barred fighting.
Moreover, to do this fighting, the Pope has a hell of a lot more
divisions, Irish, Italian, Polish, Hungarian, South German,
French Canadian, than that forlorn hope, the *Commentary*
crowd, is ever going to put in the field. I couldn't help enjoying
what might be called the Jewish style sock-in-the-eye at once
administered by Walter Kerr in the *HT*. who declared it "astonishing that so flaccid, monotonous and unsubtle a play
could be taken seriously." From accounts I've looked at it
seems reasonable certain the play is all three, and probably
because of the cheapness and false feeling inseparable from any
theatrical production, all three to a degree Mr. Kerr himself
would miss. But from his language, I'm inclined to guess that,
with an assist from his even-better-Catholic wife, Jean (I seem
to remember her saying, in connection with some overwhelm-
ingly successful, you could be sure, idiot play of her own:
something like 'the only important thing about me is I'm a
Catholic'—and, sourly (I agree) I thought; I'll bet that's no lie)
Kerr can and does honestly feel Christ couldn't have allowed
His very own Vicar to do wrong, even if it wasn't done ex
cathedra. I need hardly say such feelings defeat me. To my
limitary mind, the 'importance' Mrs Kerr assigns herself is
fantastically absurd: and Mr. Kerr's probably just in every
respect pronouncement, only suspect. Plays twice as bad (supposing that possible) could obviously, be to his mind somewhat
better if they didn't offend his preconceptions or disturb the
chip that's always on the shoulder of every literate Catholic.

III 8   *Why Writers should shut up* (con't & about time; in view of
some recent observations of mine supra). In the *Herald Trib
mag.* our Miss McCarthy pronounces: "On reflection I feel I
should tell you what I think about the very unpleasant piece
you printed about *The Group*. Like all such pieces nowadays, it
was full of mistakes as well as vulgarities. . . " [and so on & on
& on: The piece, by one Sheila Tobias, was very good in the
sense of making it appear to be a book you mustn't miss: but it
also *did* suggest in passing that from the standpoint of Vassar
women she'd talked to, Mary, at college, had been a bit of an
outsider, and the 'South Tower' girls hadn't quite realized she
and they were part of any 'group.' Mary does end by getting to
this point. "A piece like Miss Tobias', I should think, must be
much more embarrassing to the girls of the South Tower than
my novel, since in her text they appear so much more com-
monplace and disagreeable than the girls of the Group." [this

phrasing seems to leave little doubt that Miss Tobias heard and
had it right; and the cruel, though almost certainly unthinking,
brush-off of a girl, half Mick, half Jew, who just wasn't the
'Vassar type', wouldn't be affected by any amount of public
notice or later 'fame'. What, understandably, was eating Mary
then, eats her still.

III 12 Inspection of a new issue of the *New York Review of Books*
shows again the doyens of the sophomore circuit at their pretentious, labored, and far-too-long-to-read-through self-
appointed tasks. However, I read as much as I could; and there
didn't seem to be one review really going to the book itself. In
every case the nominal 'reviewer' was setting out (and always
at that intolerable length) ideas of his or her own on what the
book *should* have been if it was being found no good; or if it
was being found some good, how he or she, if he or she had
been writing it himself or herself, would have made it vastly
better.

III 14 I've been reading Gene Smith's *When the Cheering Stopped*,
subtitled the last years of Woodrow Wilson [and oh how I keep
wishing the god-awful days of the 'selling title' could get done]
which presents a lot of material new to me, a certain amount of
it, I gather, not before published. The picture, in general (the
period covered is roughly from his marriage to Mrs. Galt to his
death), is disconcerting. The last I'd read about Wilson was
Dos Passos' recent and excellent *Mr. Wilson's War* (1962)
which was about what it said it was about, not the president's
private or personal life. Smith's material certainly suggests that
the private and the personal did much to shape what was public
and presidential—a point perhaps often overlooked by histo-
rians simply because it's so obvious. At any rate, in Wilson
there seems to have been a strain, deep and wide, which if not
quite childish, was definitely non-adult. He really seemed able
to live in a solipsistic world of Scotch Presbyterian principle
which took no account of, never even knew of, actual practice.
That's about all you can say; because, alas, you very soon
realize this same Mr. Smith is not to trust. Some presumably
native imperception appears early and stays late. He doesn't for
a minute practice to deceive: his collection of fact is obviously
painstaking; but when he comes to add up, he keeps letting you
see he's constantly missing the significance of what he's telling
you. The effect is aggravated and even perhaps often oc-
casioned by a horrible style which wavers between gee-whiz
journalistic and outright lump-in-the-throat emetic ("There
was no escort for him who had known escorts for eight years of
his life" p. 187)
[Pondering this minor disaster and deciding as always it was
really kindest to not acknowledge the publisher's free copy, I

turned the book over and saw various endorsements on the back: one; "with psychological insights, with scrupulous command of data, and with a style that is alive and copiously specific without ever being cheap etc, etc": and, alas for my long professed unconcern about critical abuse I know I have to expect, it would both untruthful and useless to deny the feeling of temperate satisfaction that came over me when I found this utter critical nonsense—well: 'command of data' might be allowed, as long as you noted it was an imperceptive command—signed: Dwight MacDonald [He did the Jewish-American hatchet job on me in the little-mag. *Commentary*. It's true, I keep forgetting; but it looks as if I'm no better than the rest of Us Fellows when it comes to forgiving. Just remind me: and I'll be sore all over again, and start some mental picketing with my placard: *Unfair to Cozzens*

III 16   a passing crack in the TLS correspondence column about Somerset Maugham's style being 'cliché-ridden' reminds me of a point a wonder more and more about the longer I read and write. Could it be that the cliché is 'bad' only when the writer has nothing, or merely the stupid or obvious, to say and the clarity and simplicity of clichés instantly exposes the fact? Twistings and novelties in language can certainly delay (and for some people, what seems to be indefinitely) any recognition of such thinking basically vapid and action basically false as the later work of James Joyce sets out. But if what you have to say is worth saying, and what you want to show is the truth about life and men, the well-chosen cliché, short, quick, familiar to everyone, certainly may, as I seem to remember Maugham himself quietly suggesting, be the good, right way to convey clear meaning.

III 28   General MacArthur's, by Modern Medical Science made obviously God-awful, bowing-out seems, even so, unlikely to drag on much longer and the we-shall-not-see-his-like-again stuff is jumping the gun a bit. Certainly the story, if ever dispassionately examined, must make one of the most amazing yet lived or written. Surely no military or even public figure can match that record of being wrong, of failing, of boasting and bragging and not producing, and yet managing somehow to gather to himself all the credit when others, repairing his mistakes, checking his follies and correcting his errors, won the Japanese war in spite of him; and at least averted the total disaster his Korean plans seemed designed to ensure. As far as I can read the record, the one and only real success he enjoyed was ruling occupied Japan; and you wonder if this was anything but perfectly natural. The Orientals would expect, respect, and almost love the brag and the pose, the lifelong concern for saving and making face; with virtue and valor not a matter of what you actually did, but of what you could persuade people to believe you had done.

IV 1   *Theory & Fact.* Having duly lived my three score years I find myself apt to agree that if you believe the worst of anyone and everyone in this life you'll more often than not be right, dead right. But in fact, this is hearsay evidence. It's a conclusion based really altogether on what I learn (by reading) of this disclosed and that exposed. But if I consult my personal experience, what I know of my own knowledge, what in law I'd be qualified to testify to, I can't cite an instance to support the idea. It's just in theory that you can't trust anyone; in practice, there's almost no one you can't trust. Reviewing my personal experience I have to see and say that though, alas, I undoubtedly did other people dirt, I can't recall a case of I myself really being done dirt—that is: a blameless and innocent I by any human being done out of even the smallest of my just deserts. The fact seems to be that as far as their circumstances allow, people in general tend to be and would prefer to be kind, generous, and honest. No doubt this is even true of myself. I suppose that is, or ought to be, enough to warn me that you must of course keep an eye on those allowing 'circumstances'. They *can* alter cases: but even when they do, they are exceptions by which the rule seems pretty well proved.

V 6   In a rather nasty *TIME* review of Hemingway's *A Moveable Feast* which seems to be some posthumus fragments about his times in Paris [it was also, briefly, my time [supra IV 7]* though I never had anything to do with the Artists & Intellectuals] a point is made that I'd long thought myself alone in holding: "The reader may notice a peculiar thing about the way people talk in the book—like Hemingway characters, in fact. Some characters—, in or out of fiction, did learn to talk this way, reproduce such dialogue; but that was later. Yet here they are, in the early 1920s before a Farewell to Arms was ever written, talking like etc"
[the point was that I couldn't understand how anyone who ever listened to people actually talking could accept the generally accepted critical canon that this was good, true reporting, the way people *did* talk: and all writers of fiction must make their characters talk that way—or else! The matter was of course 'brought to my attention' by occasional criticism of dialogue passages of mine which reproduced with I think accuracy talk I knew I had heard as 'unreal'. I was puzzled until I realized suddenly that what was meant was that it didn't sound a bit like Hemingway's dialogue. It had to be 'unreal'.

*Notes on Cozzens's friends in Paris during his stay there in 1926. Ed.

V 16   *Anglican Review* comment on the late C. S. Lewis credits him, I think very rightly, with embracing S. Paul's concept [Eph. 6. 12] that "we wrestle not against flesh and blood, but against principalities and powers". Though so obvious, the point's one that never struck me before. It seems a good guess that the gist of the 'Gift of Faith' is some special capacity to see things in such terms. I have to confess that, not being of the religious temperament, I can't conceive of doing it, or of how the hell it's done. But clearly some people *can* do it; and if you can there'd be very understandable exhiliration in the idea you're at Armageddon and battling for the Lord against principalities and powers, no less.

V 18   Various comments on the Hemingway *A Moveable Feast* [supra V 6] impelled me to the prudence of doing no more than getting it from Joe Dewar's lending library; and I'm afraid it's fairly to be described as a Horrible Experience; and 50¢ for First Week is too much for it. Though, in a way, that isn't true. If nothing human is alien to you, it's very well worth reading. H.'s gift for self-expression is no mean one, and the clarity and convincingness with which he makes you see that half-highschool-kid half natural-born cheap-bastard he was in Paris in the '20s, and which, singularly enough, he managed to remain all his writing life, is instructive if rather depressing. From the introductory note, by his obviously imbecile last wife, it appears to have been done recently, perhaps his final work and that dreadful phony 'simplicity' of style was never in fuller flower: "I was learning something from the painting of Cézanne that made writing simple true sentences far from enough to make the stories have dimensions I was trying to put in them. I was learning very much from him, but I was not articulate enough to explain it to anyone. Besides it was a secret."

V 26   Pope's phrase: 'a person much bemused in beer' occurred to me for no particular reason last evening when bemusing myself in it. I sat reading Walter Jackson Bate's *Keats*. I could see the phrasing was perfect. Us beer-drinkers, when we've put down whatever our quota is, just sit there, content. You're not in the least befuddled or otherwise mentally disabled. You're not stirred as hard liquor in the amount you begin to 'feel' may stir you, to ill-advised action and general getting into trouble. You're less than jubilant perhaps: but you feel fine. Every prospect pleases. All looks well in some indeterminate, yet completely reassuring and confidence-inspiring way. Indeed, it *does* do more than Milton can to justify God's ways to man. With a beer mug beside you, it's now whatever o'clock it is, and all's (for the prolonged moment) well.

V 28   Reading Professor Bate's *Keats* (which is certainly the kind of job they can call 'definitive; but I'm afraid the vast labor of making it that makes it, or much of it, less rewarding reading than his really brilliant *Achievement of Samuel Johnson*) brings me to remember (uncomfortably) that in the summer of 1924 I was busy (along with working on a second 'novel' and a few other projects equally ill-advised) in excerpting from Keats' letters to make a volume to be called: *Keats on the art of Writing* for something William Stanley Braithwaite projected (just as ill-advisedly) as (I think) *The Imperishable Series* — reprints of the sort he planned to have Brimmer put out.* My idea was to, I guess, cull from the letters expressed views of Keats on his own and other writing and I did, as I remember complete a cutting out and pasting up of the text for which I'm afraid I may also had drafted an introduction explaining why many of Keats' observations were good and true and how a lot of points he made ought to be heeded by all writers. I suppose it's well for one to remember such things: but it's also pretty painful.

[Yet what sort of overweening self-esteem do we see here? Who wasn't all kinds of an ass when young: and what's there about me to make me feel I ought to have been an exception—or, at any rate to wish I didn't have to remember what I can remember?

*Cozzens's edition of *The Criticisms of John Keats on English Poetry Selected from his Letters* did not progress beyond the dummy stage. The preface is reproduced in James B. Meriwether's *James Gould Cozzens A Checklist* (Detroit: Bruccoli Clark/Gale Research, 1972), pp. 16-17. Ed.

VI 11   L. Rust Hills of the *Post* chosing to pay so fantastically for two short stories of mine* in order to print them before *Children & Others* appears ($4000. apiece) drives me to guess it's true—reading as a form of passing 'large circulation' time, is definitely out and these last-chance measures of desperation, amounting really to betting the stack on some one-in-a-thousand chance actually go to prove it. The confident good judgment of the editors of 20, indeed 30 years ago who did not want those stories even at the (at most) $750 price they could have got them for reflected their opinion that the boobs who bought in the magazine, the people their advertizers needed to reach, wouldn't much like them. Today, those readers are all watching TV and it's childish to suppose that people who might like the stories are or ever could be numerous enough to interest advertizers.

*"One Hundred Ladies," *The Saturday Evening Post*, CCXXXVII (11 July 1964) and "*Candida* by Bernard Shaw" (25 July 1964). Ed.

VI 15   I've been going through some *Dover* reprint volumes of H. G. Wells' stuff — collected short 'scientific' stories and novels — and I must admit to a growing amazement at the sustained,

you can only say, excellence of his writing even in the occasional evident pot-boiler or slightly tiresome (the wonder is,
it's never more than slightly tiresome) propaganda piece or
selling-job. It's certainly hard to see today how he ever could
have come to be eclipsed, indeed almost extinguished, by
writers so much less able, so much more tiresome, so vapid in
matter and so affected in manner as the Virginia Woolfs and
D.H. Lawrences. The point no doubt's simply the matter of
fashion or vogue. Woolf and Lawrence were 'new', 'different'
(that is, then: how old and hackneyed they seem now) and not
for everybody. Whether their writing as writing had merit, or
whether they had anything worth reading to say would be
quite aside from *that* point.

VII 8   With much interest I've been looking at a copy of *Holy Cross
News* VOL III NO 1 April 64 (leftover copies, one gathers,
going to a mailing list—possibly the *Living Church's*—in, well,
aid of the added building they're about to construct.) Featured
on the front page is a photograph of participants in the Life
Profession of a new Fr. Schultz and a new Fr. Ryan. This
includes, as well as the suffragan bishop Boynton of N.Y., a
good-looking coal black Brother Boniface who served the mass
as subdeacon ("the rite was performed within the context of a
Solemn High Mass"—pretty tough P.E. sledding, one must
guess). Br. Boniface would seem to show O.H.C. isn't a bit
behind the times; and elsewhere in the issue are notes on the
need for the new building by the Master of Postulants who has
23 applications for the coming year, and 38 more for the year
after. Of course 'testing your vocation' is one thing and being
professed something else: but I must admit to a feeling I can
only describe as bewilderment. Who can such postulants be?
What are they like? How do they get that way? In the case of the
Roman church, you can see that there's a tremendous 'status'
appeal to poor boys (and girls—who're also assured of life-long
support without having any 'marriage debt' to bear some lout
maybe a dozen children to get it: and even then it's almost sure
to be nothing like as agreeable and complete support 'sister'
gets in the nice new convent). Conceivably some 'Episcopals'
find something psychologically rewarding (though certainly
not 'status': just as laymen, they have all the Church can
provide of that already) in the regular life; but being P.E.,
there'd seem to have to remain implicit a 'doubiousness', a
not-quite-the real-Roman-thing element, an unconvincingness
of mere imitation, that you might think those temperamentally
inclined that way must find dissatisfying.

[of course, I must allow for my own total incomprehension. I
simply cannot understand how anyone can possibly support a
belief (and, moreover, one that you can hardly doubt is

wholehearted in a great many cases) in a (to me) patently preposterous supernatural 'religion'. How in God's name can good sense live with an acceptance of such a story as that of the Atonement? This may be a crazy world: yes: but as crazy as that? Damn it all: no!

VII 18   Margaret Culkin Banning sent S. a copy of her new novel: *The Vine and the Olive*. It seems to be intended as a protest, though always devout and gentle, against the Roman stand on contraception. It is not in any way a good book: but it's also not in any way a stupid or 'bad' book. The general effect is the somewhat dismaying one of honest childishness perennially triumphant. You're a little perplexed, when you remember how long Mrs. B. has been writing and how much she has written, by the obvious inefficacy in her case of exercise and experience—she somehow doesn't learn, hasn't learned to write, as one is supposed to, by writing. Despite her years, she also remains serenely enough not-grown-up, mysteriously insulated from actual life. I don't mean she's unaware of, or refuses to acknowledge any of those 'facts of life' which go to her theme. She recites them dutifully: yet without any apparent realization of what they must add up to in reason: and so without the insight which might let her make real and plausible her young newspaper-woman-protagonist. Her mental and emotional situation—she is awfully intelligent and realistic: she is awfully Catholic too—is perhaps somewhat unusual but, our human nature being what it is, just slightly improbable— far from outright impossible. But Mrs B, I suppose, naturally, doesn't think of going into this, the one part of it (the why and how of this) that could catch and hold readers of adult intelligence. She just you might say posits it; and with an earnestness, a trying-hard that makes you feel like patting her on the head, prattles away.

VII 20   Christopher Hassall's *Rupert Brooke* makes curious and rather uncomfortable reading. Presumably it's uncomfortable because the conclusions you're forced more and more to come to aren't welcome. The young man and his 'set', those friends with whom he stays, or who stay with him at his mother's place are introduced in a way that seems to have a certain fair promise—these people are agreeable and intelligent. But as you read on (the book is good in the sense of being fully and carefully detailed and documented) some doubt gradually enters. They are all too evidently posing most of the time: they are too much interested in making themselves 'different'. If Brooke and Virginia Stephen (later Woolf) swim in the nude together it's not because of any possible incentive to copulation it's because it (as they might have said) cocks a snook at stuffy proprieties. (I can't help feeling it would have been better for both of them if the practice had been incidental to or associated with that right true end of love). I suppose this usually no more than slight but incessant phoniness sums itself up in the 'war sonnets'. I know several by heart because, as on most people, they made a great impression on Landon Robinson, then teaching me third form English at school. 'Now God be thanked who has matched us with this hour' is in content really sheer crap with none of the perhaps silly but still true truth of 'I could not love thee, dear, so much / Loved I not honor more'.* If you set: 'If I should die, think only this of me' against 'No longer mourn for me when I am dead',† a sort of flimsy mawkishness both in thought and wording is distressingly clear.

*Richard Lovelace, "To Lucasta, Going to the Wars." Ed.
†Shakespeare, Sonnet 71. Ed.

VIII 30   In connection with one William Goldman's *Boys and Girls Together* which the publisher sent me, and which I find pretty hard going of that twice-read kind. You tell me what your characters do, but to get me to accept them is 'people' your job as a writer is to make me understand how they came to do it. Saying they do isn't enough, particularly when you say they do things that common experience suggests aren't likely unless you haven't described them correctly. It won't do, this way. [while I think I'm probably right in judging the book to be pretty bad, I must remind myself that my feeling that Jews writing about Jews are too many and getting to be too tiresome can perfectly well have all the 'unfairness' that I see in the Jew Boy Liberal Intellectual gang-up on me. *Children and Others* has just brought a couple of new 'attacks'; so now I'm doing it, too?

[that kind of critical or literary enuresis

9   22 October 1964-8 April 1965

XI 1   Gordon Haight sent me a copy of George Eliot's *Middlemarch* which he had edited for Houghton Mifflin's Riverside Edition and I've been reading it with some interest. There's indeed that need to get used to the language but even when you've done that (not hard, if you're used to reading Shakespeare and so have experience in thinking in not exactly another but a variant idiom) there seems to me to remain—the situations in *Middlemarch* emphasize it—a great difficulty in the Victorian conventions which ruled out any mention of sexual fact. Obviously it is of the first importance in understanding the described course of events to know, say, whether Mr. Causaubon was (as seems possibly hinted) impotent; and, if he wasn't, what kind of a lay he found Dorothea; and what pleasure or lack of it she found in carnal connection (or lack of it). When the relationship is reported without any reference to what the average reader's ordinary experience makes him know to be a very important factor in how marriage works out I think he is apt to feel a certain un-realness in the author's recount, a want of the candor with which he ought to be treated when he is asked to accept what he reads as true experience.

[Middlemarch p. 178 "The theatre of all my action is fallen. . ." Yes, how rightly put. What does a man do then?

XI 7   Reflecting more, (and reading more) on *Middlemarch* (supra XI 1) I'm struck by that business of the effect of the out-dated style as an instant impediment to today's reader—the turns of phrase seeming affected, the idiom hackneyed. You must read on far enough to get used to it. You then, I find, tend to forget it, not notice it. As soon as this happens you discover—you're apt to be a little rocked-back—that fiction's one end, aim, and reason for being, the conveying to the reader of thoughts and pictures from which he may take that new acquist of true experience, is being served not just as well but much more fully, more informatively and instructively than modern modes, like those of Virginia Woolf, James Joyce, Henry Miller, or Norman Mailer ever get to serve it. Their surface is (or was— highbrow regard for that sort of stuff has certainly not yet ended, yet one feels a developing loss of enthusiasm, a sort of checking or wondering in the literary atmosphere) 'modish'—the right word, I think—but their once novel deviations in 'style' now no longer arresting, ebb in interest to leave high and dry the vapid content, the phony substance, the untrue experience, the solemn-ass pure nonsense they once hid—though did they ever deceive anyone who had real discernment; or who wasn't young and uncertain and so afraid to say he couldn't see what he was told magisterially he must see, or be despised? (I speak here of myself forty years ago). At any rate, under George Eliot's by time made un-modish surface of style what you find is sound observation and solid sense, stuff worth reading and worth pondering

XI 9   Though [*Middlemarch* again] I have to leave open my doubt [supra XI 1] It is raised by the p. 427 mere reference in passing—". . . leading finally to the loss of her baby." Though sexual factors then impossible to state are sometimes, though unmentioned, conveyed better than you'd think possible, I'm not satisfied that getting to the point afterward in this fashion can substitute for the course of writing clarity and sense which would have required Lydgate to say: Now that you're pregnant, horse-back riding could be risky. Of course I can see that the phrasings used may well have told the reader of the 1870's what the case was, just as if you said a female was indisposed, it would be understood that she was menstruating—but, on the whole, no. If any fact is pertinent, state it exactly in plain words.

XI 12 *The Curtis Publishing Situation.* I'm still being bombarded (almost) with notes from various Sat. Eve. Post editors suggesting I do pieces on this or that for them and though the notes are 'personal' there is that in their form suggesting if not hundreds, at least dozens, of writers regarded as established are being simultaneously importuned. By continuing reports of internecine corporate warfare in the WSJ it seems evident that these are SEP's desperate and violent death-throes (like Mr. Hills' purchase last spring of 2 stories of mine for $4000 apiece) and editors simply feel they have nothing to lose because all is lost There are points of interest in this decline and fall from the days of the Independence Square building's erection (I never saw it until the late thirties when the relatively vast lobby with its Maxwell Parrish murals and playing fountains had an absurd, dated look, very different from what you could be sure had been the look of artistic elegance they started out with) and the length of a generation's settled, seemingly permanent, prosperity to the first cracks and saggings after Lorrimer's death when for some years it was plainly felt it was only a matter of getting the 'right' editor—if not Wesley Stout, why Ben Hibbs—and nothing was seriously wrong. Things are clearer now. Lorrimer's creation rested on a contriving to present for five cents a good supply of reading matter of a kind a cut above 'the pulps'. This, though far from 'serious' literature, could not be supplied by ordinary hacks. You had to pay at rates that would make really practiced professionals, authors of published, best selling books anxious to write for you. What it came down to was an amazing, even brilliant juggling act. The reader paid five cents (I seem to remember that in the late 'twenties the Post actually cost Curtis about twenty cents a copy) to read the writers he liked to read, and once it was clear which writers produced the right material they were paid more than any writers had ever been paid before. Now came the advertizers, persuaded—and for years it would seem quite rightly—to pay all the staggering Curtis deficits in preparation and production of the Post and a fat profit for Curtis besides to get their copy before the readers who got what they liked to read for, from their standpoint, almost nothing. On the face of it, the operation was fantastically unsound. The forever irrevocable laws of supply and demand were violently violated. The article on sale cost many times as much as it was being sold for. You weren't turning out something for which there was a demand at a price that meant a profit. What you were really selling was not a magazine, the Post, but advertizing space. Once the demand for that weakened, you had nothing at all, you were out of business. The present frenzied efforts to make the magazine 'appeal' to more readers are manifestly vain— you have to make it 'appeal' to more advertizers, and up against TV, plainly you can't hope to.

XI 14   In Somerset Maugham's *The Summing Up* [one, I come to realize, of the mere handful of books of our time that remain and seem likely to remain really profitable reading] which I was leafing through to check something else (I couldn't find it) I came on his comments p. 76 et seq. on talent, genius, and the 'greatest writers', one of which he says he sees he cannot hope to be, 'never having felt some of the fundamental emotions of normal men' etc. This may be true, but considering it, wondering if much more can be told you than he tells you so lucidly and well, I had to wonder suddenly if those 'greatest writers' today tell anybody much of anything, because I must suspect that very few of them are generally read. Outside academic circles where reading them may be a professional chore, are Homer, Dante, Cervantes, popular reading anywhere? Is Shakespeare? In my desk-rack of books I have a battered copy of G.B. Harrison's Complete Works* and probably there isn't a day (a matter of habit) when I don't (but idly, of course) read a little here or there. That can't be called really 'reading', and I must wonder just how many people ever look at a line of Shakespeare, let alone ever settle down and read a whole play through.

*Of William Shakespeare. Ed.

XI 16   Still in that matter of Shakespeare (above) it must be said he is being 'produced' everywhere and all the time in a way utterly unimaginable when he was alive and I don't think this could happen if it was done always or even often at a subsidized loss. Of course plays of his are free in the sense that you don't have to pay *him* anything, but if adequate parts of the 'public' didn't want to, or couldn't be cajoled into thinking they wanted to, go to them, production, one guesses, would pretty quickly peter out. I can see that it may be a matter of my own temperament that makes this amazing to me. All the Shakespeare I've ever seen produced—and, young, I used to see all I could—seemed to me simply ghastly. When I read him, following the dialogue and watching the described action in my own mind, it was nothing short of electrifying and indeed often still is. Things

are, if not always, at least an amazing most of the time, put so
effectively, said so damn well, you feel a kind of tingle of pure
pleasure and wonder. The intrusion of actors and actresses to
mouth it in make-believe, the certificate of phoniness given by
footlights, 'costumes', grease paint and canvas props simply
(for me) destroys all value or values. I cannot sit through it:
everything is made not just stupid or dull, but piercingly,
intolerably boring.

XI 20   Long (and much too long) half-frustrated—no: make that:
wholly, not half) frustrated in my efforts to do what I want to
do in my still, in spite of the years and the reams of writing gone
into it, inchoate *Morning, Noon and Night* I decided some
back it would have to go into the 1st person which (I'm sure I
can't think why) seemed to release me at once (so far at any
rate). I thought I'd better check on the technique in several
effective 1st person novels I remembered and had around, one
of them being, of course, H.G. Wells' *Tono Bungay*; and while
it's irrelevant to my reason for rereading it I was driven again to
wonder how it was possible for work so full of the basic virtues
of all good writing—the vigorous clear prose, the effective
excellent strokes of close observation and lively imagination,
the constant insight of good sense to fall quite out of favor in
'serious' criticism which for years persisted in ascribing Real
Merit only to what was confused, fuzzy, phony, and hard to
read—the last, particularly important. The defection seemed to
get its start with D. H. Lawrence and Virginia Woolf, go on to
ordain Ezra Pound and James Joyce geniuses and to continue
though evidently weakening in absurd claims for writers (at
least if they write on modish subjects) who write about as badly
as possible today. Why? [or is perplexity here just ingenuous? Is
anymore reason needed than the itch of 'intellectuals' to prove
that's what they are—not as other men, and the going along
with them strictly the emperor's new clothes stuff?

XI 28   Proof for something in something called 'contemporary writers'* (I think) though taking a fairly bright view about me
quoted some of the Jewish critics on my alleged defense of 'the
upper classes' against, presumably, *them* (I often wonder if any
of them sees what, if this were really the case, he would be
tacitly conceding). I have admitted before and I still admit that
it's very hard for me to understand how anything I ever wrote
supports them in this, any more than how anything I ever wrote
can reasonably support them in what they really mean by all

Contemporary Authors, vols 11-12, ed. James M. Ethridge and Barbara
Kapala (Detroit: Gale Research, 1965), p. 95. Cozzens's response to Chester E.
Eisinger's claim that he "defends the status quo" and asserts "his approval of
its essential character" was : "This is just plain crap. I don't defend anything; I
don't eagerly assert anything."

their crap—that I'm antisemitic, and want to run Jews down. I know that any—well, pontificating, on the subject of yourself is always shaky. You don't see yourself. Yet, in a sense, you *feel* yourself, and I know I wouldn't be anti-anybody by category or class for the bad (not good) reason that this would involve by definition some subscribing to or standing on principle; and I really have no principles. I don't give a hoot in hell about the race, color, religion of individuals. All I go by is whether I find this one agreeable—or, in short: if he be not bad to me, what care I how bad he be?

XII 12   *Elizabeth Taylor's* new book does not come off too well (*The Soul of Kindness*) but she is a really good writer and in a way that seems to make it hardly matter whether the book 'comes off' or not. I mean; a reader's time is well spent with what she writes, no matter what. I think this comes from an astonishing, hard to analyze, capacity she shows to convey convincingly what it's like to be a woman. I've never seen any writer do it as well, or even nearly as well. You find yourself inside the feminine mind looking out — not, as the case seems usually to be even with women writing about women, just the female observed: her outward appearance painstakingly presented, her behaviour carefully described. You're shown exactly how the fact of feminity controls and colors her thinking: you're made to see (and to quite understand) the 'reasons', to her so good, for acts that may strike a man as altogether crazy, or at any rate and at best, completely incomprehensible. Of course it can remain an open question whether she really has it always right, whether this is actually how it is; but her writing job is done to the hilt when she contrives to make her reader, often both startled and illuminated, hesitate never an instant over the argument of her narrative. [cf. VOL. 2 III 9]*

*Comments on Taylor's *In a Summer Season* (1961). Ed.

I 8   It's one of the commonplaces of everyday observation that the more sensitive, that is, the 'touchier' a man is himself, the more regardless he is of other people's feelings. He'll seldom hesitate about doing to others the very thing he would not have done to him: and in this connection I suppose it might be guessed that the man who doesn't get sore easily or often is probably insensitive rather than well-balanced or self-controlled. Ordinarily when you say 'man' in this use you also mean 'woman': but pondering the point, I find myself wondering if there isn't a difference, if for some reason, a 'sensitive' woman (S. is very much one), though quick to feel resentment at wrongs done or supposedly done her, is as a result (except when repaying the specific wrong) better able to be sympathetic, and through active awareness of how *she* would feel, apt to be unusually regardful of other people's feelings.

The Human Condition. It is January and half past nine at night with snow (though less than we often have) covering the ground, and several degrees below zero outside. But, indeed, ha, ha, we are warm in my mellowly lighted study with its agreeable walling of books, and 21 original small folio framed Currier & Ives Civil War Prints, and a lot of pretty good hybrid African violets flowering in ranks on window shelves; and I sit at my desk perusing (right word) Dangerfield's *Chancellor Livingston*, reading about as agreeable as possible, with a mug of Miller's High Life beer at my hand (it is true that I would prefer National Premium from Baltimore, if only I could get it) and my Cervantes cigar supplied me by my Mr. Silverman of Peterson's Ltd and though made in Tampa, still all Havana (it is true, I would prefer one of the no longer obtainable Romeo y Julietta Numero 57's) and am I content? By God, perfectly! Is this the best of all possible worlds? Well, at this minute, it is for sure. It seems right to put this acknowledgement on a record in which I seem to do a good deal of carping.

I 19   A note in the *Harvard Alumni Bulletin* correspondence along with some passing remarks in the *Williams Record* going to the recent 'parietal rules' business, or Girls ad Lib. vs. Girls Limited in bachelor quarters while still giving me slight starts of incredulity, have undoubtedly that fait-accompli tone that suggests all argument about it has ended—or at least nobody remains to lift a voice about it being 'wrong' or 'immoral'. The point of continuing interest to me here is that though having girls when they could be had never seemed to me in the least 'wrong' or 'immoral' any habitual having of them (I can remember a couple—and I mean two only, of my college acquaintance who whored around fairly freely) did seem to me improper—that is, vulgar or in very bad taste and I suppose subconsciously at least still so seems to me. I cannot think why. Though I can see that lack of opportunity, or when opportunity existed or could easily have been created, timidity was largely responsible for my mostly 'chaste' conduct at college I'm not persuaded there was any sour-grapes element in my seeing 'bad taste' in frank and open tail-chasing (then the phrase for it). I think I really did feel there was some 'grossness' about it—something for whatever reasons psychologically repellant in a way entirely unrelated to any concepts of 'wrongness' or 'wickedness'. This seems the more perplexing, for I was of course the fairly regular masturbator most youths of my then-age are; and why I saw my own private practices as more refined I don't know. [unless, of course; because I could keep them 'private'—pretend, in the passive sense of giving it to be understood they weren't mine, that I didn't; while those inclined to 'tail-chasing' may have been apt to give it to be understood they did more of that than they did.

The 'scandal' at the Air Force Academy which seems likely to involve the 'resignation' of perhaps a hundred cadets, though at first made something of a mystery, now seems to go, as a couple of years ago here at Williams a difference of opinion went, to the utility and propriety of an 'honor code' having to do with 'cheating' on examinations. The great majority of the AFA's possible hundred delinquents don't appear to have done any 'cheating' themselves, but apparently conclusive evidence (I would be interested to know what it was and how it was obtained) came to light showing them to have been well aware that steps were being taken to help athletes maintain scholastic grades high enough to remain eligible to play. The wording of the 'honor code' is given as: 'We will not lie, cheat, or steal; nor tolerate among us those who do.'
[One, or at least I, can only say: No, No, No! You have done enough if, considering it to your spiritual or other advantage you do not allow yourself to cheat, lie, or steal. You may properly cherish or even coddle your own 'honor'. Integer vitae scelerisque purus pleasures or advantages are personal, your own business. You are simply a common informer, a quite low form of cheap bastard, if you are able or willing to do any of that not-tolerating. I think it says something good for our often unpraiseworthy human nature that many young men rebel, won't stoop to obey any such orders.

II 5

Omne ignotum pro magnifico—and why not? If you treat as 'great' what afterwards is seen to be little it may be slightly embarrassing: but if you treat as little what turns out to be 'great', as a judge or critic you've really cooked your goose.

II 6

Air Bombardment Air Marshal Sir Robert Saundby [a very good historical job] "Their experiences of being bombed had inclined the British to put [1943] rather too much emphasis on the moral effect among the civil population of heavy air attacks. Insufficient allowance was made for the degree of control over the population exerted by the authorities and police in a totalitarian state." [the wonderfully unemphatic statement arrested me because it is the first time I have seen even indirectly admitted what *Top Secret* material shown me, as I remember by General Vandenberg, in the Pentagon in 1944 seemed to make clear. The fact apparently was that while the German air bombardment had done very little serious damage in the physical sense to the real British 'war potential' one of the greatest mistakes Hitler made was in swallowing as he or his intelligence services must have, the British propaganda line about the universal stiff upper lip, the Londoners' cool and collected 'civil defence' work, and their, by accounts, almost jolly herding daily or nightly into shelters. The reports I saw maintained that this had been really true only to start and only for a couple of weeks. After that, 'morale' in the civilian population as an entity steadily declined, and by the spring of 1941, just before the German General Staff or Hitler himself decided to abandon the night attacks and use the forces that had been allotted to them in the Russian venture was on the verge of a collapse which, if bombings had just been continued on the established scale and schedule until June, was virtually certain to have been total. Or, exactly as Sir Robert suggests, British 'authorities and police' would have been by training and tradition quite incapable of keeping the civil population in line the way they could be and were kept in line in Germany under air bombardments that made that of London and other English cities seem hardly more than token.

II 15   Brandt & Brandt sent up two quite heavy filing cartons of 'business correspondence' about stuff of mine going back to 1925 and a leafing over of it does present points of interest & instruction. It is, for instance, hard now to remember with what fervor I pressed to get myself published anywhere, anyhow; and how much (of course, futile) use I made of calculated brag and bluff with the idea of inciting Carl Brandt and 'Miss Baumgarten' to greater efforts on my behalf. Perhaps the principal thing to be learned or noted is the very full evidence given of the near impossiblity of making anything like a living if you are a 'beginning' writer and of the very little you'd better be prepared to make even when you're 'established'—that is, with a number of published books behind you—unless you happen to be the beneficiary of one of those quite inexplicable 'breaks' that are visited rather less than one a year on some single scribbler among the thousands and thousands. The individual's chances would seem to be (and differentiated in no way I know) about those of hitting a slot-machine's jackpot. Certainly if you consider the real 'best-seller' count through the whole past generation you can't (as is also the case in the awards of Pulitzer and all other 'prizes') imagine the matter of merit, of 'just deserts,' has anything to do with it. A good book *may* get the break or the prize but the ratio of such gettings is perhaps about that of good books to bad books—say, one to one hundred. Maybe, if differences in taste are allowed for, an entirely 'bad' book never gets either; but books little or no good can and do get either or both practically all of the time—

II 22   one of those always odd-ball critical curs to be found without fail snapping at the heels of any writer whose book has sold in a really big way.

III 2   *Sobering Thought?* in re the '1000 pickets' the denial of tenure to Yale professor of philosophy 'popular 32 year old Richard D. Bernstein' it seems hard to doubt that the thousand Yalies, rather than being roused by strong feelings either about philosophy teaching or professors just hadn't had such fun since Grandma caught her tit in the wringer or the academic equivalent: and one Professor Sewall, Master of Yale's Ezra Stiles College spoke as a real boob in saying to 'a victory rally of 500 students' [the dean or the president, apparently disconcerted into witlessness, agitatedly proposed to 'reconsider'] "Even if B. is denied tenure once again, a far-reaching precedent has been set. There is no nook or cranny in the university now into which the spirit of the demonstration has not penetrated. You have created a sense of Community at Yale" [But of course if Prof. S. is really right about that, and the policy of the administration is to be determined by undergraduate whim and demonstrations for the hell of it, he may be real smart in moving to make his own nook or cranny as habitable as possible

IV 6   A magazine called *Ramparts* which I never heard of before, but which must have been around since the copy I'm sent says: VOL 3 NO. 6 MARCH 1965 seems to be published (and in point of format, on no mean scale: there has to be plenty of money behind it to turn out that kind of 'book') by something called: The Layman's Press in California which as nearly as I can make out is a group of 'Catholic Liberal Intellectuals' (Surely like Newton's Infidel Astronomer they have to be Mad?). Perhaps as good earnest of their 'liberalism' a lot of their staff seems to be Jewish, among them, Maxwell Geismar, working in their book section who directs an attack (of all things) on Saul Bellow's bestselling *Herzog* which certainly in venom and for all I know in stupidity goes even beyond the *Jewish-American Commentary* attack on me by, I think, Dwight Macdonald. [It was: I just checked a copy I kept in my Kick & Nut file—I thought for a moment it might have been Norman Poderentz, the editor, who has also always been plenty anti-Cozzens]. I'd forgotten about that matter; but remembering it now, I'm afraid I find myself feeling a quite nasty sort of pleasure in what the *Commentary* matter must have driven (and drives: let me not kid myself. I may forget all about it for months, even years: but when I remember, their spleen — Macdonald & his MacCult and MacCrit — is my spleen) me to regard as dog eats dog— ie. Jew chews Jew. I know it's greatly to my discredit (and I mean what I regard as discredit to me; the only 'discredit' I ever seem to give much of a damn about) but there it is. I haven't read any of Bellow's work recently since what I did read seemed to me dismally bad— which is to say, of course, not the kind of work that I get anything out of and even I can't imagine that's definitive in re. good or bad. The point of most interest to me had however nothing to do with my ill-natured Jew-chewing-Jew satisfaction. What Geismar was making at some length perfectly clear was that still hard for me to credit truth about the fancier little-mag reviewers and any book not to be classified as 'popular fiction' that sells really well. That is what they can't stand: and the at first glance too-simple explanation of why they can't (G. titles his piece: *The Unbearable Bellow*) I find myself obliged more and more to admit is the likeliest. Probably not one of them ever set out to be a 'reviewer'; they all set out to be 'writers' (like the people they're now reduced to 'reviewing') but they had no, as they would regard it, luck; no one would pay them enough to make a living for their 'original' work. Since very little 'original work' does pay much, this may be most of the time relatively 'bearable'—if they have regular reviewing jobs they're probably paid more than nine out of ten 'serious' novelists make. But, oh my, if some 'serious novelist' is seen suddenly to have made, or to be to make, a fortune! Unbearable is the word for that, all right. Or as G. revealingly puts it: "... I regard the reception of this book [*Herzog*] as the great literary scandal of the year. All I can do to console myself [Yes: that's the word, chum] is to remember that Mary McCarthy's *The Group* had the same reception last year, and both of these novels, I think, are complete sell-outs, and both these writers, by now, are completely commercial and corrupt."

[the perhaps dismaying thing is that you can be sure he manages to be unconscious of, or at least adequately to rationalize, that rage of envy that finds or invents the faults he wants to see. This is a brave blow struck for 'truth'. This is, as MacD. had it I remember about me, a dedicated stand against the lowering of all literary standards.

10   15 April 1965-31 March 1967

V 4

In the latest batch of those 98 cent (or so) remaindered books I seem unable to stop ordering (though we are bursting with books already) was G.B. Stern's *The Way it Worked Out*. An English writer of moderate note (and little merit) of more than (it must be) thirty years ago, she had, I remembered seeing some back, turned papist. [Query: has anyone of great or real merit in any line of endeavor ever turned papist? Well, there's Evelyn Waugh, certainly a writer of merit: but I must suspect that what I've told was his homosexuality keeps him from being a valid example. Converts always do seem to have to have something 'wrong' with them—a need and hope to be comforted, to escape situations that kept causing them emotional distress]. However, Stern by photographs of her, was big, homely Jewish girl [could that have been her 'private ail'—physical unattractiveness?] who didn't seem the type to kid herself so I remember feeling a mild (an uninterested) surprise at the time. How would it work out? perhaps a Sheed & Ward 'slim volume' on the subject suggests a possible protesting too much, but by the account given, it seems in that wonderful fun & games way to have worked out fine. The ungraced infidel must of course gape & gape (or pinch himself) at the relation of the standard pleasures so seemingly factitious and 'difficulties' quite unconvincing, so obviously unreal in labored overstatement. She does her best to make out that it isn't all beer and skittles (dreadful loss of spiritual and intellectual face) but at least to someone of her essentially childish temperament (Our Lord did say once and for all the real last word about the kingdom of heaven) that's exactly what it proves to be. [and of course it was that temperament that made it impossible for her, write and write though she did, to write anything worth an adult's reading.]

V 7   Anne Ford of HM sent me John Braine's new novel *The Jealous God*. He is competent and literate (always a slight surprise and great relief these days) but his characters happen to be north-of-England Catholics of Irish extraction and serve to rearouse in me that amazement mentioned above. Because of the competent and literate writing you are well enough persuaded that these are possible people, that they feel, think and act as represented—he makes you, you might say, see them doing it. The story-line, adequate without being in any way seriously 'compelling' has to do with the relations of a young secondary school teacher (of locally substantial family) with women and his relatives. One of them is the wife of a brother of his; one, a divorced protestant girl (and, though nothing prevents him from having sexual intercourse with either, he can take a wonderfully matter-of-fact, almost business-like attitude. Since, naturally, he doesn't want to risk remaining too long in a state of mortal sin, he'll confess and be absolved before Easter, but meanwhile—well, nihil obstat. The protestant girl's divorced husband ends by killing himself, and how much the young teacher's relations with her had to do with it involves some ethical introspection—need he or need he not confess to murder?—but the main point is that marrying her has been made possible, and he appears to purpose to do it.

V 12   I have been looking at W.A. Swanberg's *Dreiser* (Scribners) which, appropriately enough, has Swanberg's facsimilie signature in gold on the cover, for while the book and the writing are both inferior to that in Ellmann's *Joyce* and Shorer's *Lewis* this is definitely another of those I can't but feel ironic instances of a book *about* an author and his writings much more worth reading than anything the writer himself ever wrote.

V 14   Swanberg *Dreiser*. You can't read very far in Mr S's account (documented with a care I would think the greatest I've ever seen. This may be what works against, to some degree, qualities of 'readability,' in which as noted above I found him falling below Ellmann and Shorer [I suppose, a point of sorts. If you bind yourself to show 'proof' about every statement you make can you hope to have your reader impressed by your facility in discernment and in expression?] that D. was, on the evidence so fully and fairly offered, beginning almost at his beginning, in almost every way just so plain 'awful'—a natural-born cheap bastard: actively dishonest whenever he got an opportunity to be; stupidly and grossly undiscerning whenever discernment was called for; and voluminous producer of perhaps the worst English prose that has ever yet found itself printed and bound in books.

V 15   Swanberg *Dreiser*: As the narrative proceeds, you are led to understand (Swanberg is good about this—he doesn't tell you: he shows you) the ingenuous truth underlying a literary 'reputation' surely as spurious as any that ever once obtained. It really all boiled down to the then problems of 'censorship.' D's 'greatness' as a writer consisted in his 'boldness' in occasionally mentioning sexual matters. This is not to make little of the 'boldness'. He would write as he saw fit, and if the self-appointed 'vice societies' got his books banned, so be it. He would not agree to excise a line or change a word. All liberal thinkers found this stand excitingly admirable (and indeed none of us who writes is unindebted to him. That stand was to make possible today's freedom to be honest in prose fiction) but in their excitement many of them plainly managed to make themselves blind (Not H. L. Menken, it would seem. While sharing the excitement and forcefully supporting the 'stand' he never claimed D. had any merit as a writer or a novelist) to the fact that unexcised lines were as execrable as all the other lines, and that the unchanged words were no less 'unjust' than all the other words. [This goes interestingly to the matter of careless and inexplicit writing as an unfailing sign of falseness and phoniness in what is being written. If every word of it isn't explicit and clear—not to be confused with clear-and-simple: in this life the simple may tell some truth but it never tells anything like the whole truth—don't believe a word of it.

V 28   More Thoughts on the Swanberg *Dreiser*.
the record so carefully documented suggests that D. managed

to go beyond Joyce, S. Lewis, Fitzgerald, and Hemingway in sheer awfulness as a person or human being. Yet there were those who if few, perhaps fit, were evidently able to remain attached to him. In some of the as described rather repellent women he you can only say used a pecuniary interest seems possible. Apparently he was never as poor as he made himself out to be, and finding this out, the various more or less ill-favored wenches involved with him may have hoped to latch onto caches of cash they might have imagined larger than they were. On the other hand, he seems up to the last year of his life to have remained a more or less compulsive whoremonger and while this might have been some form of prostate gland trouble that kept (as Gibbon quotes Mohammed's as being) his penis always pointed toward heaven and did not mean potency and actual performance, there are occasional passages in letters quoted to and from some of the women that suggest, preposterous as his public representation of himself as a 'great writer' may have been, in private representations of himself as a great cocksman he delivered the goods, gave females the best of possible reasons to be 'attached' to him.

VI 18   Guy Chapman *A Passionate Prodigality*. For some reason Holt, Rinehart sent me a reprint of the 1933 recount of 'World War I' experiences and I have to agree that it's worth reprinting in that you get a very good picture of 'daily life' in trench warfare of 1916 and 1917 and of course, though far from agreeable, it was a life you see both between and in the lines not by any means intolerable; and lethal, as far as most of the combatants went, only in a limited, not too frightening way. Most of the blood and guts crap (Mailer, Shaw etc) put out after 'World War II' was so palpably phony no one outside the sophomore circuit (where actual inexperience could accept getting kicks out of, 'realism' the more unrealistic the better) would be likely to take it as any kind of true experience; but, I can't quite pin down my 'sources', I had somehow gained and never lost the impression that the Flanders trenches were sheer unrelieved hell and the over-the-top actions out of or into them matters of mass murder. The point of interest is human credulity. If you have average intelligence, you must as an adult have learned something of life and men. The accidents of war may throw men into forlorn hopes, catch them in slaughterings they can't get out of—but never all the time or even often. No great numbers of them can be made to stay where they don't feel reasonably safe. You can't lead or drive them into situations where death is clearly certain. Mr. C.'s batallion did indeed end decimated, but the process was gradual, never too-scaringly relentless and regular.

VIII 12   Perhaps a little tardily in its book columns *The Living Church* turns up with a review of *Children & Others* which seemed to me of some interest the Rev. & PhD. reviewer* observes: 'Of late many critics have seen fit to attack Cozzens because he doesn't say what they like to hear, or doesn't say it in the way in which they would like to hear it said, or both. . . The sensible reader will seek the facts. He will turn to this latest publication and discover for himself whether or not the writer can entertain, inform, perhaps even enlighten him. I think he will render a favorable verdict on all counts. . . Perhaps the ten stories that deal with childhood and youthful experience are the most moving The never-faltering details and the never-failing narrative honesty make them the finest stories I have read in a very long time. They yield rich pleasure, they satisfy as only good writing can, they have the look of durability.' [This of course says to what can fairly be called perfection what anyone serious about his writing wants to hear. To this reader he is getting across just as he hopes to and struggles to. The point of interest is of course that I *am* saying what *he* would like to hear and saying it in a way *he* would like to hear it or both. I can't but see that this goes directly to some matter of overtones in phrasing, word connotations, impossible to-nail-down conveyings of indefinable attitude in what I write that must account for that on the face of it inexplicable fury the 'liberal intellectual' Jewish critics visit on me. Something sets their teeth on edge. Even when nothing is said that could remotely involve them they can take themselves to be disprized. I must guess it is because my scenes seldom fail to be those into which they cannot see themselves fitting and my people are almost entirely those they have reason to feel they couldn't get to know, indeed those by whom, at one time or another, they have been most hurtfully—and also, as likely as not, most unfairly—brushed off. My L.C. reviewer, to the contrary, recognizes himself as fitting in perfectly, as having known these people all his life. Of course what I say about them has that 'look of durablity' to him. Of course what I say about them has, to the stung attackers, the look of lousy writing. Worth remembering, I think.

*William Turner Levy. Ed.

X I   After many too many hesitations I've been steadily going ahead with *Morning Noon & Night* for the past weeks. It is not what I wanted [and what exactly I wanted I can't say—only: something more than this: no doubt what Marlowe in *Tamburlaine* meant in that passage: "Yet should there hover in their restless heads/ One thought, one grace, one wonder at the least/ Which into words no virtue can digest] but plainly I must accept my limitations and settle, in place of what I would want to do, for whatever I prove able to do. But a plain effect of it is that I'm moved much less frequently to note here things I note, think of, or remember. My face shot off in the morning, I'm silenced or nearly silenced for the rest of the day.

X 20   That seamy side of human nature. You must be careful how you treat people as your equals. The average person has much more respect for you if, even though he resents it, you make it plain to him that you consider him of no great importance. The line may be a thin one, but if you're 'nice' to him beyond what he, perhaps subconsciously, feels are his deserts he will much more often than not despise you for it.

XI 4   Symptom of Age? I'm troubled a little to find that people who aren't bores at all, now, if I spend any length of time with them, quite quickly tend to bore me. I have to see the horrid possibility that it won't be long now until I find no one interesting but myself. *There* I seem to feel no flagging of interest.

XII 25   Aldous Huxley. (Preface to: *Art & Artists*) "there is no equivalent in literature of sustained counterpoint or the spatial unity of diverse elements brought together so they can be perceived at one glance as a significant whole" [But one seems to want to keep trying. He made the point himself in regard to his *Eyeless in Gaza* in the course of a lunch I had with him and Denver Lindley I guess about nine years ago. It impressed me. I made a mental note that someone far abler than I am conceded it couldn't be done even by him. But still I seem to have to go ahead with 'Morning, Noon, and Night.' I can't stop trying to do what I see very well I'm not going to succeed in doing, and what I know I'm foolish to attempt.

I 10   talk of new 'forms' of the novel makes me make a note that perhaps under the title of: *A Time of War* a book could be put together from my own diaries in the service and the stuff in my Pentagon 'memoranda' with comment on what I did not write then, or what I see today.*

A Time of War (Columbia, S.C. & Bloomfield Hills, Mich.: Bruccoli Clark, 1984).

I 15   The quality of mercy is so well regarded that one usual fact about a showing of it goes as a rule unobserved (It just occurred to me). Any 'justice' that looks better or juster with a seasoning of mercy can't have been ever very 'just'. Around the edges of most exercises of soft-heartedness is (what a thing to say: yet consider carefully) a margin of slop. The merciful man, searched, is much too often going to be found to be here or there soft-headed—he suffers, when he does good, loves mercy, yet most of the rest of the time from natural silliness.

I 20   I have been looking again (I saw without favor some of it in the New Yorker) at Truman Capote's top best selling *In Cold Blood* (a 'new' form of the novel, he and everyone else says). So it may be, but I must feel the form's possible merits or virtues are hopelessly obscured by what I rightly remembered as the writer's faults as a writer. In *thinking*, he is obtuse; in *feeling*, he shows that distinctive and destructive imperceptiveness of native sentimentality which has defaced so much of the last 30 years' seriously-taken fiction. This makes his values keep ringing false. He patently misinterprets many of his facts. His judgment about motivation and interest doesn't compell your assent. It is mostly blurred a little or muddled a little. He does not know, he has not learned, enough about life and men, to realize the actual meaning of what he's telling you. It grates on you more and more — like off-key singing, or news reporting—a more exact parallel—by a novice radio announcer. To estimate the 'new' forms possibilities you have to see it handled by a writer of the technical competence and the intellectual calibre of a, say, Somerset Maugham. [one must wonder if a man of such abilities would ever need to, or feel he needed to, look for 'new' forms.

IX 3   In his *Literary Horizons Sat. Review* column Granville Hicks who manages to mention me quite frequently (no doubt because of a 'monograph' on me he is doing for the University of something or other* which he wrote me about early this year asking if I wanted to say anything: I said no) speaks of 'the present-day crisis of values' of which most 'contemporary novelists to whose work (he) is attracted' are acutely aware. "James Gould Cozzens and Louis Auchincloss are exceptions, and that is why I am uneasy with their writings though I admire their craftsmanship and respect their integrity. Both of them it seems to me are writing their novels as if the world in general and the Western world in particular had not gone through a dozen revolutions in the last half century. Cozzens makes a strong case for common sense as the solution of many human problems, but he refuses to look at those problems before which common sense is bankrupt. . ." [This kind of thing really beats you and I'm certainly 'uneasy with' Hicks' writing as a critic when he makes it so plain that to a novelist attentive to his duty it can't matter a hoot in hell how many revolutions the world has gone through. He has no business looking at 'problems' or offering solutions to them: his proper study is mankind, how men are seen to act and so seem to think. Noting and reporting on that is a whole time job and if he doesn't confine himself to it, while he may attract the momentary attention of our Granville Hickses, he's unlikely to write anything really worth reading.

James Gould Cozzens (Minneapolis: University of Minnesota Press, 1966). Ed.

IX 16   In my earnest efforts to make myself regard nothing human as alien to me I think I do pretty well but much that's human is sure tiresome as hell.

IX 30   *The translation problem.* I have just had copies of *Kinder &* *Andere Leute* Sigbert Mohn Verlag "Die Übersetzung aus dem Amerikanischen besorgte INGE LINDT" and I was amused to find that with my general knowledge of the text in English the German became remarkably readable and I could even spot translation devices and recourses mildly instructive or amusing. You see to start that in German 'and others' won't serve. You expand to 'andere Leute' to be good German. Then there are such problems as that of homonyms. My Laura says in English: *John is my only beau* but in German that has to become 'mein einziger Verehrer'. In English John, not understanding, can think of 'bow as in bow knot and bow as in bow and arrow'. In German the translator can only interpose: 'Ich wusste nicht recht wie sie das meinte.' Difficulties often occur with idiomatic & allusive titles: *The Animals' Fair* becomes '*Eine fortschrottliche Schule*'; *Total Stranger*: *Ein völlig fremder Mann*: *Every Day's a Holiday* is: *Whisky Verboten*. The point would indeed seem to be that in translation all shades of meaning disappear and if you're saying or trying to say anything more than: the cat sat on the mat it won't be conveyed when put, however painstakingly, into a foreign language.

XI 9   My pen pal Wm Buckley kindly sends me, inscribed, a copy of his *The Unmaking of a Mayor.* I read dismayed. He manages (and not stupidly at all) to give 'conservatism' all the earnest humorless obtuseness and self-defensive compulsive tendentiousness of any Little Mag. run-of-the-mill 'Liberalism'. Phony as any Liberal. I will of course swallow dismay and write him some approbation

XI 12   In *MNN* what I want to do is present stuff in a form of true experience, the happenings of living life as I have found them to happen. That is: living, you keep being confronted with facts, things as you discover them to be. Sometimes right then, most often a good deal later, explanations may (or may not, of course) come, showing you, letting you realize, how it happened, why it happened, or even, what really *did* happen (at the time, you may not have been knowing enough to know).